"I suddenly feel as if the scales have been lifted from my eyes. You truly demonstrate how understanding the language unveils so much about the culture."
— Carol Potter, Executive Vice Chairman at Edelman

"A lively and original approach to navigating the bottomless mysteries of Chinese language and culture. Stewart Lee Beck is a knowledgeable guide on how to understand China better, and how to have fun along the way."
— David Brooks, Chairman,
Coca-Cola Greater China and Korea

"With humor and clarity, Language Empowerment *weaves together rich cultural and linguistic background information of the Chinese language with practical implications for daily communication."*
— Michael Volz, Chinese Program Coordinator,
University of Missouri

"China Simplified does an excellent job demystifying what can often feel like an impenetrable place. I wish a book like this existed when I moved to China."
— Dan Washburn, Chief Content Officer, Asia Society;
author of *The Forbidden Game: Golf and the Chinese Dream*

"Totally authentic. I am encouraging my local Chinese friends to read this book to understand how to more effectively relate to non-Chinese speakers."
— Christine Ng, Managing Director, BBH China

"Katie and Stewart have done a great job of pulling together all the best ideas that are shared by China lifers and putting them in a book. It's fun, but you'll also be far better prepared for the challenge ahead."
— Owen Caterer, Founding Partner, Caterer Goodman Partners

"They've cracked the code! China Simplified demystified Mandarin for me, and now many of my clients."
— Mary Rezek, Executive Coach and Founder, Saatori, Ltd.

"Having lived in China for nearly 20 years, I found myself nodding in agreement throughout the book. The authors grasp very well that their audience varies from expert Mandarin speakers to total newbies. Well done!"
— Mark Secchia, Founder, Sherpa's Food Delivery

"I love China Simplified. What I would have given for this no-nonsense, elegantly simple advice on China when I was there."
— Louise Ardagh, Head of Small Business at Bankwest

"An entertaining and easy read with a twist of humor. I've learned an enlightening cache of information about the country, its people and its language from a non-native speaker."
— Paul Chin, CEO, Bacardi Greater China, North Asia & Oceania

"Language does indeed offer a key to the gates of China. This book makes people feel like an Old China Hand in a flash!"
— Rudi Messner, Partner/Director, Zotter Shanghai

"This book should be required reading for every foreigner before getting on the plane to China."
— Miao Jun, former HR Director, Asia-Pacific, Milliken Inc.

CHINA SIMPLIFIED

Language
Empowerment

Demystify Chinese culture
and fire up your Mandarin

Written by
Stewart Lee Beck and **Katie Lu**
Artwork by **Aaron Gu**

In memory of
Zhou Youguang, the Father of Pinyin
1906 – 2017

© 2017 China Simplified, Inc.

www.chinasimplified.com

Portions of this book have appeared in different forms on China Simplified and other online platforms. This book was previously released in e-book and audiobook formats under the title *China Simplified: Language Gymnastics*.

For more information, please visit www.chinasimplified.com.

ISBN 978-0-9960950-3-7 (paperback)
ISBN 978-0-9960950-1-3 (digital mobi)
ISBN 978-0-9960950-5-1 (digital epub)

Also available from China Simplified:
China Simplified: History Flashback

"Complexity is your enemy.
Any fool can make something complicated.
It is hard to make something simple."

— Richard Branson

"To attain knowledge, add things every day.
To attain wisdom, remove things every day."

— Laozi (Lao-Tzu)

"Learning is the only thing that the mind
never exhausts, never fears, and never regrets."

— Leonardo da Vinci

CONTENTS

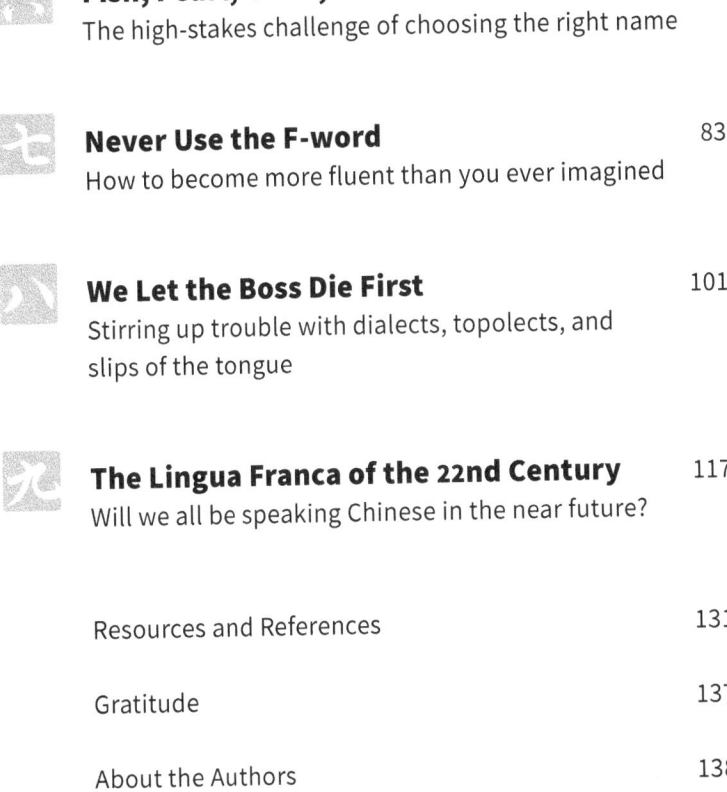

Why China Simplified?

The journey began with a series of questions we couldn't answer: Why do so many people seem to know so little about China? What is it about China that intrigues us, and captures our imaginations? And, with all that's been written and said about it, why is China still so misperceived and misunderstood? This was the genesis of the China Simplified project.

China Simplified explores and demystifies the country and its people for the rest of the world. By shifting our collective attention beyond the 1% (hot-button issues in the mass media) to the other 99% (relevant conversations about history, language, business, and more), we hope to raise cultural awareness and increase mutual understanding.

Be Careful What You Wish For

I didn't arrive in China speaking advanced Chinese. Far from it: I came here with zero, zilch, nada.

My dream-in-progress was to learn Portuguese and Spanish in South America, but I was interrupted by an unexpected detour to East Asia. On that trip, I made the spontaneous decision to sell everything and move to China. That was 25 years ago.

Chinese characters intrigued me from the moment I immersed in the culture. I headed to the local bookstore and bought a two-inch thick "portable" paper dictionary with characters so tiny that even an ant would need glasses to read them. I sensed this was going to be a long, hard slog.

One of my early Chinese language classroom experiences in Shanghai was with two Japanese students who could read most Chinese written characters, yet spoke nearly incomprehensible Chinese. I remember thinking: if two of China's smarter neighbors are struggling to *speak* a language they can already *read*, how could I, a neophyte Westerner, ever expect to speak decent Mandarin?

Then something miraculous happened. I gave up. I stopped trying. I surrendered my fight against the language and committed myself, every time I studied, to find something entertaining, unexpected or intriguing in the universe of Mandarin. In short, I started having fun. That little change of focus made all the difference in the world.

> *"You don't learn a language, you get used to it.*
> *You don't get good at a language, you get used to it.*
> *You're not bad at a language, you're just not used to it."*
>
> — Khatzumoto

Unless you aspire to make your living as a translator or in professional broadcast, attempting to learn to speak, read, and write perfect Chinese from scratch as an adult is a venture in futility. Most people quit, which is sad because buried somewhere in all that frustration is the spark of genuine interest. And that, my dear readers, is what this book is all about: sharing my many personal disasters (and a few triumphs) to help make the Chinese language and culture more accessible to a wider audience.

Stop Laughing, This is Serious

Five years ago, I told my Mandarin teacher, Katie Lu, that I wanted to write a book with her. She nearly fell off her chair. As a language professional, Katie overflows with talent and enthusiasm for her students, and, well...let's just say I wasn't on her short list for most likely to succeed.

I explained that many of my overseas friends are curious about China, yet still perceive the culture as impenetrable and the people as inscrutable. My plan was for us to collaborate on a fast-read book full of lighthearted stories, that is, to use the language as a window into the culture.

Much later, after she read the first draft, Katie told me something that made all the work worthwhile. She said, "I never knew my language was so beautiful."

"The illiterate of the 21st century will not be those who cannot read and write, but those who cannot learn, unlearn, and relearn."

— Alvin Toffler

The actress Helen Hayes once said, "The expert in anything was once a beginner." So my best advice for language students at any level is: let go of your fear and persevere, and have some fun along the way!

The future of our world is interconnected with that of the people of China. Wouldn't it be great if we could all communicate a little better with one another?

Stewart Lee Beck
Shanghai, June 2017

Foreword

My first real job in China, 11 years ago, was as academic director and host of a language-learning podcast called ChinesePod. Each podcast contained a short, practical Chinese dialog that helped learners communicate information crucial to daily life in China. But simply covering the vocabulary and grammar was never enough; what gave ChinesePod its charm was the way we delved into the culture behind the language, through the lens of our own individual experiences. Although we saw ourselves as language teachers, I came to discover that some of our listeners, far from being on the fast track to fluency, were listening precisely for the cultural insights. For them, it wasn't about building a massive vocabulary or achieving one hundred percent comprehension; it was about the direct human connection made possible through the language.

China Simplified: Language Empowerment is all about the experience: enabling you, the reader, at any skill level, to get more benefit and pleasure from speaking Chinese. This book is not a textbook or a language course, however. Authors Stewart and Katie impart plenty of encouragement, spinning story after story about the many pitfalls of learning Mandarin, and urge you to forego the paralysis by analysis which holds back many students.

> *"The authors are the grinning pilots who take you up in a plane for a good look at the lay of the land, and then ask you to jump!"*

— John Pasden

For many future language students, this book will mark the beginning of a lifelong adventure into the rich terrain of the Chinese language (or better said, *family* of languages) which is as unique and varied as the land it embodies. And just as you can't see every part of China on your journey, you can't expect to learn the language through books alone. Mandarin itself offers a stunning array of territory any learner can delve into, even with only a smattering of words and phrases as a starting point. And that's the key, isn't it? To get started somewhere.

No matter whether you're already serious about your Chinese studies, or simply hope to improve your cultural awareness before your next interaction with Chinese friends, *China Simplified: Language Empowerment* will point you in the right direction. It provides just enough knowledge for you to be dangerous, and entertains you the whole way. This is precisely how any good China adventure should begin: with a big smile on your face.

John Pasden
Founder and CEO, AllSet Learning
Shanghai, June 2017

The Sound of Somebody Falling Down

Why Mandarin is the easiest (and hardest) language in the world

船到桥头自然直。
Chuán dào qiáotóu zìrán zhí.

The boat will straighten before it hits the bridge.

Chinese is the easiest language in the world. Think I'm full of *gŏushĭ* 狗屎 (dog droppings)? Read on and I'll explain why.

Imagine a galaxy far, far away, where everyone uses much simpler grammar: nobody bothers with singular and plural, masculine and feminine forms don't exist, tense variations are a breeze, and there are no complex verb conjugations. Sound too good to be true?

In English, groups of animals are so complex even Dr. Seuss gets migraines. There are gaggles of geese, armies of ants, glints of goldfish, hedges of herons, leaps of leopards, murders of magpies, lounges of lizards, mischiefs of mice, movements of moles (pause, deep breath), prickles of porcupines, pods of pelicans, parcels of pigs, plagues of locusts, prides of lions, riots of bulls, schools of sharks, kettles of vultures, beds of oysters, crashes of rhinoceroses, rhumbas of rattlesnakes, and (my favorite) implausibilities of gnus. In Chinese, it's a piece of cake: *yī qún* 一群 (one group) for all of them.

Verb conjugations are much easier in Chinese than Romance Languages. Yeah baby!

To Be:		To Go:	
shì	(是, am)	*qù*	(去, go)
shì	(是, are)	*qù*	(去, go)
shì	(是, is)	*qù*	(去, goes)
shì	(是, was)	*qù le*	(去了, went)
shì	(是, were)	*qù guò*	(去过, have gone)
shì	(是, will be)	*qù*	(去, will go)

Note: the letter 'q' in Pinyin is pronounced 'ch'.

Widening your Chinese vocabulary is not that hard, thanks to the romanized version of the language called *pīnyīn* 拼音 (lit. "spelled sound"), which gives a direct phonetic shortcut to any character. Pinyin was specifically designed to raise literacy rates and help learning-impaired foreigners like me more rapidly reach advanced stages of ineptitude.

The Significance of Tones

Mǎ māma mà mǎ māma ma?
马妈妈骂马妈妈吗?
Do horses' mothers scold (other) horses' mothers?

The smash success of Pinyin in raising literacy and spreading the language is due in large part to a Changzhou man named Zhou Youguang (周有光). An economics professor and former banker who speaks Japanese, English, and French, he's most famous for his prolific work as a language explorer. At age 30 while traveling abroad, Zhou met Albert Einstein, who told him: "Your life ends at 60, so that gives you 13 more years for work and 17 more years for leisure. Whether or not you are successful depends on how you use your leisure time."

Zhou returned from overseas to create Pinyin. However he got caught up in the Cultural Revolution and ended up in the countryside, not returning to Beijing until 1984. In 2005, he published a new work at age 99 and proclaimed: "This will not be my last book!" True to his word, he kept writing, and published *My Life Story* in 2013 at the ripe old age of 107.

A poem by Zhou reveals his outlook on life:
My bedroom is my kitchen, which makes eating
  convenient
My bookshelf is my kitchen cabinet, that makes my
  books smell good
My door is falling apart, because I have lots of guests
My floor is uneven, but welcoming to those who want
  to dance.

Oh, and I forgot to mention that Chinese can be a lovely sounding language. Not when I speak it, but that's beside the point. Many refer to Mandarin as the "French of Asia" for its singsong flow, a comparison more evident when listening to music videos than when haggling over the price of vegetables.

Chinese respond with unbridled enthusiasm to others learning their language. I kid you not, here's a typical opening conversation almost anywhere in the country:

Me:	*Nǐhǎo!*
	你好!
	Hello!
Local:	*Nǐde Zhōngwén shuōde hěnhǎo!*
	你的中文说得很好!
	Your Chinese is great!
Me:	*Nǎli nǎli. Wǒ zhǐ huì shuō yīdiǎndiǎn!*
	哪里哪里, 我只会说一点点。
	You're too kind, I can only speak a little.
Local:	*Āiyō! Tāde Zhōngwén zhēn lìhài!*
	哎呦!他的中文真厉害!
	Wow! His Chinese is truly amazing!

My Favorite Mistakes

What I meant:
*Nǐ de **xióngmāo** hěn kě'ài.*
你的熊猫很可爱。
Your pandas are very cute.

What came out:
*Nǐ de **xiōngmáo** hěn kě'ài.*
你的胸毛很可爱。
Your chest hair is very cute.

Note: the letter 'x' in Pinyin is pronounced 'sh'.

No doubt you picked up on the uncanny similarity to giving your French a try on the streets of Paris. To say the Chinese *lǎobǎixìng* 老百姓 (common people) appreciate their foreign guests struggling with their native tongue is an immense understatement. There is an honest respect—coupled with plenty of polite exaggeration—for those persevering with a language which even they, as native speakers, consider daunting.

Don't stop now—we're almost at the start

At this point, you might be thinking: Hmmm, maybe Chinese isn't so hard after all. And that, my dear reader, is where our *folie à deux* ends. When I said Chinese is the easiest language, I was also politely exaggerating. Here comes the other side of the story, unvarnished.

Chinese is harder than most languages because of one word: tones. With a slight warble of the voice, the exact same phonetics in Pinyin can have a totally different meaning.

Expert Opinion

We've been studying together for over six years, but it's still really hard not to laugh when Stewart makes a complete verbal disaster in Chinese. I have to pinch myself real hard to kill the urge to crack up and with a totally straight face say, "Close! Would you please try again?" As a teacher, I have to remain encouraging and professional at all times. But trust me, just because I've traveled to twenty countries and he's lived here for twenty years doesn't mean we always understand each other.

Messing up the four tones of Mandarin—commonly referred to as *pŭtōnghuà* 普通话 (common language) or *hànyŭ* 汉语 (the Han people's language)—is as easy as falling off a horse while its mother scolds you. For even more sophisticated blundering possibilities, you might try Shanghainese with its eight tones or Cantonese with its nine. More on them in Chapter Eight.

To be clear, Chinese is more a family of languages than a language itself. We wouldn't ask anyone, "Do you speak Indian?" We ask them if they speak Hindi or Tamil or Urdu or Gujarati. Likewise, many Chinese people speak more than one of the 80+ recognized dialects of Chinese. That said, Mandarin is the standard dialect in Mainland China (and across much of the globe), which is why we've chosen to focus on Mandarin with simplified characters in this book. Many of our observations also come from a China-centric perspective, though we appreciate that Chinese everywhere share traditions and some sense of connection.

One of the many likeable things about conversational Mandarin is if you forget a tone and guess "up" (e.g. using 2nd or 3rd tone which both rise), you've got a 50-50 shot at being approximately right. Clever way to slide by, huh? I thought so too, until I smashed head-on into a short story revealing the true need for greater precision. First, here's the English translation of the tragic story of Mr. Yi:

> Yi's aunt died and left him billions. Yi went to town and asked a doctor to inspect the real cause of his auntie's death. The doctor did the checks, but on the second day, the auntie's money went missing. Yi suspected the doctor took the money and expressed his doubts. The doctor hanged himself to prove his innocence. Yi began to think in his chair about the loss of billions and wronging the doctor. So Yi hanged himself as well. So sad! This is so damn weird!

Now, here is the same story in Pinyin and characters:

Yī yí yì, yí yì yì. Yī yì yì, yì yī yíyì, yī yī yī yīyí.
伊姨殪，遗亿镒。伊诣邑，意医姨疫，一医医伊姨。

Yì, yì yìyí, yí yī yǐ yǐyì. Yī yǐ yíyí, yì, yǐ yí yī yí.
翌，亿镒遗，疑医以议医。 医以伊疑，缢 ，以移伊疑。

Yī yǐ yǐ yǐ yì, yì yǐ yì yì yí, yǐ yì yī yī, yì yì.
伊倚椅以忆，忆以亿镒遗，以议伊医，亦缢。

Yī! Yì yì yǐ!
噫！ 亦异矣！

Awesome huh? Every single character in this improbable tale is pronounced "yi." Written in characters it's crystal clear of course, but when read aloud, the story is only comprehensible if the listener follows its tones and context. In fact, the universe of same-sounding Pinyin also includes *jian* with 221 characters, *fu* with 226 characters, *yan* with 237 characters, *zhi* with 248 characters, *xi* with 268 characters, *yu* with 291 characters, *ji* with 305 characters, along with the aforementioned *yi* with 370 unique characters. Good thing we don't have to memorize them all.

Tones aside, reading and writing characters is the biggest challenge. It's also what makes Chinese endlessly fascinating. Those fluent in several Romance languages, who then study Mandarin, often conclude that characters are what give the language its intellectual depth and cultural connectedness. But that doesn't make the learning process any easier! You may need to write the characters a lot to remember them. And that's often the deal-breaker. Sad to say, it's far too easy to give up and reach for the video game.

It's not uncommon for foreigners on their China journey to feel that nearly everything in the East is expressed in a manner opposite to the West. The language differences are countless and begin to influence how you think about the people and how you experience the culture. It gets into your skin. For those who summon the tenacity (or the lunacy) to fully embrace and flow with the language and culture, the myriad of differences is exactly what makes living in China so enchanting.

Spot the difference?

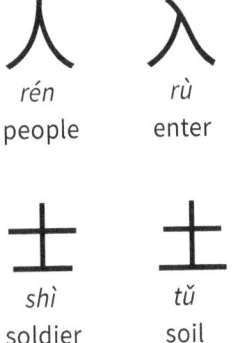

人	入
rén	*rù*
people	enter

土	土
shì	*tǔ*
soldier	soil

白	自
bái	*zì*
white	self

未	末
wèi	*mò*
future	end

Even the Chinese themselves can struggle with writing the harder characters. There's a story I enjoy about a young Chinese, poor like many students, who found himself wandering past a noodle shop around lunchtime. He heard people inside saying *"biáng! biáng!"* to order noodles, and feeling quite hungry, entered to see for himself. The student watched the cook pull long strings of noodles and serve fresh bowls of them to satisfied customers. Excited, he asked for one.

After scarfing down the bowl, he realized he had no money to pay the bill. The cook flashed him a look. Sensing trouble, the student thought fast.

"What do you call your noodles?"

"Biángbiáng noodles," replied the cook.

"Do you know how to write the character *biáng*?"

The cook scratched his head, having never thought about it.

"Then I'll teach you how and my noodles are free!"

Before the cook could protest, the student grabbed some paper and wrote a character so complicated that everyone in the restaurant burst into applause. The cook smiled and tore up the student's bill.

The cook's noodles soon became legendary. That's how everyone started using the word *biáng* to imitate the sound of someone falling down and feeling surprised, just like the first time Homer Simpson bumped his head and exclaimed, "D'oh!"

In other common versions of the story, *biáng* comes from the sound of a cook slapping noodles against a table or the sound of people munching the noodles. Less important than the origin of the story is what it says about the language and culture.

Sinologist Victor Mair of the University of Pennsylvania in his blog *Language Log* explains it this way: "For me, *biáng* symbolizes the difficulty of accommodating the full fecundity of folk, popular and logical/regional cultures and languages within the bounds of the standard writing system, which enshrines the elite, high culture, and now also the bourgeois, urban, national culture. In other words, *biáng* is well-nigh bursting at the sides of the scriptal and phonetic boxes within which it is constrained."

Not bad for a character that likely sprung from the tangled imagination of a noodle cook centuries ago in Shaanxi Province, China. *Biáng* is hands down the hardest Chinese character so fortunately for us, every character we encounter in the future will seem easy by comparison.

The character *biáng* requires 62 strokes to write it. Good luck guessing the correct stroke order!

A Picture's Worth
Ten Thousand Words

The mystical origin of characters and East-West perspectives

肉包子打狗 有去无回。

Ròu bāozi dǎ gǒu, yǒu qù wú huí.

If you throw a meat bun at a dog,
don't expect to see the bun again.

Characters are the window to the soul of Chinese culture.

Chinese characters are the oldest continuously used system of writing in the world, dating back to 6,000 BC cliff carvings found in the Yellow River Valley, one of the cradles of civilization. More recently, around 1,100 BC, oracles in the Shang Dynasty Royal Court etched symbols on turtle shells and cow bones to divine the future. (Hmm, wonder if the oracles ever saw this literary train wreck coming.)

After shells and bones, people started writing on bamboo. And since there was an infinite supply of bamboo and eons of pent-up things to say, writing went viral. Scribbling on bamboo was also vastly more practical than say, chiseling a love poem to your soul mate on a massive bronze bowl and lugging it up the hill to her mud hut.

My Favorite Mistakes

What I meant:
Wǒ yào **chūmén**.
我要出门。
I'm going out. (lit. "I will exit door")

What came out:
Wǒ yào **chūjiā**.
我要出家。
I'm becoming a monk. (lit. "I will exit home")

You might be wondering how certain cultures ended up with an array of pictograms instead of an alphabet of letters. It turns out some early peoples valued the ability to communicate directly with an image, while others preferred a phonetic system which links symbols and sounds. The Chinese chose the former.

Successive generations of language scholars, in their prolific glee, expanded the range of symbols to support the rapid exchange of ideas. Multiple sets of symbols often coexisted in and across dynasties, becoming forerunners of the language itself.

Fast-forward a few thousand years to 1716. The Kangxi dictionary contained 47,035 characters. Parents everywhere scratched their heads and said, "Keep going, son, you've only got 32,501 characters to go!" By 1994, the Chinese dictionary had nearly doubled to 87,019 characters. More ink, anyone? And according to experts at the Beijing Chinese Character Study Bureau, there are now exactly 91,251 characters in use today.

Sleight of Hand

School kids in China must somehow learn 15 new characters per day, writing each 50 – 100 times before daybreak.

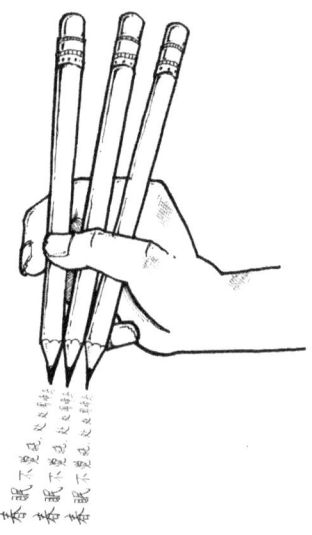

As a student, I was knocking out one new character every day with rock solid comprehension until I realized mastering them all would take centuries. I was googling "Tibetan longevity practices" when Katie confided a well-guarded secret of the trade: by learning just five characters per day, the average foreigner can reach the reading level of any well-educated Chinese person in just two years.

"Theoretically," I responded.

"Definitely doable," she replied.

A smile grew on my face.

"Even for you," she added.

Good thing I wasn't fishing for a compliment.

Expert Opinion

Don't let him scare you with writing characters. It's not uncommon for overseas Chinese to speak multiple dialects, say Cantonese, Hokkien (aka *Fújiànhuà*) and Mandarin, yet not recognize more than a handful of characters. This shortcoming doesn't seem to handicap them much when traveling or doing business worldwide, which proves you don't have to recognize a dictionary full of obscure characters to become a proficient Chinese speaker like Stewart. So how to start? Be practical. Focus first on spoken results and learn to recognize characters later, or in parallel with speaking. Language purists may take issue with this approach, and maybe they're right. All I'm saying is, if you want to speak Chinese, go ahead and start! Use Pinyin on your digital devices — it's easier than you think. Nobody says you have to learn thousands of characters before you can enjoy the language.

Fortunately for impetuous youngsters and linguistically challenged adults alike, there are only 2,500 most-frequent characters and 1,000 secondary-frequent characters, making a total of just 3,500 commonly used characters. Most Chinese will confess there are plenty of characters they don't recognize. All you need is around a thousand to command day-to-day Chinese. Starting to sound do-able? Should you choose to accept Katie's challenge of five new characters per day, which by association will teach you many useful new words, your confidence level with the language will soar.

Demystifying the phonetic/semantic character model

Phonetic:

Same phonetic on the right side of the characters hints that their sounds are similar.

Semantic:

Same water radical on the left side of characters tips off their meaning

Roughly 90% of all Chinese characters are *xíngshēngzì* 形声字 (lit. "shape sound characters") which is a big assistance to learners trying to read and pronounce them. But beware, this trick doesn't work all the time.

Some of the most seismic language upheavals came during the modernizing movements of the 20th century when vast swaths of traditional characters were simplified to boost literacy and make the language easier to learn. Kids everywhere rejoiced and went outside to play.

Most Chinese grow up learning either simplified characters (the Mainland, Singapore) or traditional characters (Taiwan, Hong Kong, Macau), but not both. Despite the compelling societal benefits of simplification, some say the process of character amputation left us with a less beautiful written language.

Electric Brain

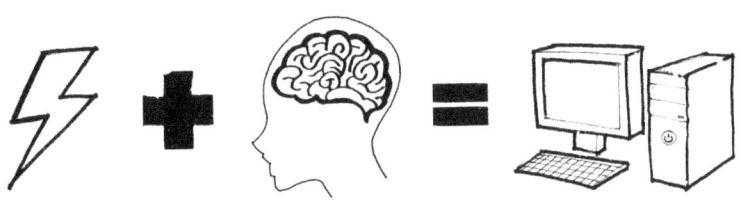

Some Chinese words originate from a combination of descriptive characters; others come from phonetic sound-alike characters:

Diàn 电 (electric) + *Nǎo* 脑 (brain) = Computer
Wēi 微 (micro) + *Bō* 波 (wave) + *Lú* 炉 (oven) = Microwave oven
Kǒu 口 (mouth) + *Hóng* 红 (red) = Lipstick
Pì 屁 (fart) + *Gǔ* 股 (organ) = Butt
Kā 咖 (brown) + *Fēi* 啡 (morphine) = Coffee
Mí 迷 (attractive) + *Nǐ* 你 (you) + *Qún* 裙 (skirt) = Miniskirt
Pài 派 (assign) + *Duì* 对 (couple) = Party
Hēi 黑 (black) + *Kè* 客 (guest) = Hackers

Perhaps this is why the art of calligraphy resonates with so many people. Form trumps function; brush strokes are appreciated for their style and flow, for the dance of ink on paper. Those who enjoy calligraphy describe the joy of getting lost in the meditation and exploring sublime subtleties. Even drawing the most basic *héng* 橫 (a short, flat, hyphen-like stroke) involves seven micro-movements of the hand to get exactly right.

Illustrating the traditional to simplified transition

Traditional	Simplified	Pinyin	Meaning
龍	龙	*Lóng*	Dragon
書	书	*Shū*	Book
愛	爱	*Ài*	Love
門	门	*Mén*	Door
桌	桌	*Zhuō*	Table
王	王	*Wáng*	King

The characters for "dragon" and "book" changed a lot; the characters for "love" and "door" didn't change that much; and the characters for "table" and "king" didn't change at all.

You can take the Chinese out of China ...

I've encountered an interesting bias in the Mainland when it comes to how Chinese perceive their own people growing up in other countries. I once found myself pulled into a discussion about how a British couple—first time to China, no Chinese skills, blown away by the experience—had just adopted a young girl from Henan and returned home to settle her just outside London.

"I hope she learns the language growing up," I said.

One of the elderly aunties in the room looked askance at me.

"Of course she'll know the language, she's Chinese!"

This charming auntie was certain the young girl, even in a faraway land, would somehow channel the language by virtue of her Chinese DNA.

Embracing the Ambiguity

Exploring the hazy space between what is said and meant

一切尽在不言之中。
Yíqiè jìn zài bù yán zhī zhōng.

Everything is inside of no words.

Westerners crave specificity and directness; they like getting to the point. "Now, please." "Don't waste my time." "For God's sake, spit it out son!"

Easterners prefer the indirect approach, talking around points of contention, seeking refuge in ambiguity to avoid confrontation, and understating themselves wherever possible. Chinese would much rather *rào quānzi* 绕圈子 (beat about the bush) than let on you're about to make a strategic error which could cost your company millions. Why deprive others of the pleasure of unraveling the hidden meaning behind their carefully chosen words?

How to mess around

Dǎo jiànghú 捣糨糊 (stirring glue) means "messing around" in common speech, though it can take on a variety of meanings based on context:

Nǐ dǎo shénme jiànghú?	你捣什么糨糊？	What are you talking about?
Nǐ dǎo le bàntiān jiànghú, dàodǐ yào shuō shénme?	你捣了半天糨糊，到底要说什么？	You've been stirring glue for half a day. What are you really trying to say?

Or when you want to get someone's attention:

Dǎo shénme jiànghú?! Zhège zěnme néng chī?	捣什么糨糊？！ 这个怎么能吃？	What the … ?! You expect me to eat this crap?

The thinking goes something like this: time is of no consequence as long as I'm filling up these moments with words, often without saying anything of substance. After all, not everything need be said between friends, and to reveal my true intentions is far too abrupt and shallow. So please, relax, be patient, and perhaps, eventually ... I'll dangle a clue about what I really want. And don't worry, if you miss the first dangling, I'll dangle again later.

If you are *hánxù* 含蓄 (humble, subtle) and able to embody and contain this depth, you are considered well-educated with refined tastes. In terms of inner substance, the more you show, the less you have.

Let's have a look at the old school orientations of a Western and Chinese businesswoman during an initial meeting in China:

Western Businesswoman Lateral thinking, direct expression. Efficiency and multitasking.	**Chinese Businesswoman** Literal thinking, indirect expression. Hierarchy and sequence.
– Oh what a lovely day.	– Are you hungry, have you eaten?
– Your city is so beautiful!	– Your Chinese is so good!
– I love your top, where'd you get it?	– You don't feel any jetlag?
– Okay, enough polite chit chat.	– We're starting to know each other.
– Let's lay our cards on the table.	– I can't let her know what I want.
– I can give you this if you give me that.	– She wants this more than I thought.
– I can't lose this opportunity.	– I don't want to rush into things.
– This contract tells us exactly where we stand and protects us both.	– This contract is just a starting point, we can renegotiate later.
– Good ... are we finally there?	– Good ... are we ready to begin?

Nowadays, many Chinese business people have a more international view, or if not, can easily switch back and forth between cultural orientations. Baked into these sweeping generalizations are the seeds of their demise. They are accurate, yet imprecise at the same time. (After all, this is a chapter on ambiguity.)

Most prominent are the values learned growing up. There are Chinesey white kids, just like there are westernized yellow kids—some of whom affectionately call themselves "eggs" and "bananas"—yet even values and upbringing don't tell the whole story.

I met a five-year-old boy from a mixed-race family who likes to help around the house. He offers his African father a beer, and if the answer is "no" then it's a no, end of discussion. But when his Chinese grandmother says "no" to a cup of tea, the boy continues pestering her until he gets her real answer. "C'mon grandma, have a cup of tea, you'll like it!" He's already mastered the fine art of the conversational flip-flop. If child labor weren't so administratively awkward, I'd hire that kid to run my company.

My Favorite Mistakes

What I meant:
Wáng xiānsheng de bàba zǒu le.
王先生的爸爸走了。
Mr. Wang's dad just left.

What they heard:
Wáng xiānsheng de bàba zǒu le.
王先生的爸爸走了。
Mr. Wang's dad is dead.

Same characters, different meanings. Just one of those you have to know.

Here's another telling conversation from a Chinese family setting:

Daughter:	Dad, can I take you to Hong Kong for your 60th birthday?
Father:	Don't trouble yourself.
Daughter:	It doesn't matter, it'll be fun, and it's your big birthday!
Father:	Don't worry about it. Let's not waste money.
Daughter:	I've already saved my salary for several months.
Father:	But it's troublesome to work out so many things.
Daughter:	Don't worry I'll sort everything out tomorrow.
Father:	So which day are we leaving?

The culturally Chinese mind considers *tí yāoqiú* 提要求 (asking for things) and *yǒu xūqiú* 有需求 (needing things) as too direct, even rude. There's also a preference for leaving room for correction, so someone might say *kěnéng ba* 可能吧 (maybe) to a dinner invitation just to keep his options open. If he later chooses to go, he can tell the hostess that he has time. If he decides at the last minute not to go, and an upset hostess is still holding a seat for him, he can fall back on his original "maybe". In other words, rudeness is subjective and ambiguity in China equates to flexibility and saving face.

Richard Nisbett in *The Geography of Thought* investigates the East-West cultural differences and concludes:

Westerners—and perhaps especially Americans—are apt to find Asians hard to read because Asians are likely to assume that their point has been made indirectly and with finesse. Meanwhile, the Westerner is in fact very much in the dark.

Here are several delicious ambiguities you may encounter in China:

Mǎshàng dào le
马上到了

Translation: I'll be there immediately.
True meaning: I'll be there sometime in the near future.
                      Probably.

Westerners talk about time to get somewhere, e.g. "I'm ten minutes away." There's often a shared view towards timesaving, at least in big cities. Chinese rarely talk that way, unless they've adopted this Western habit. *Mǎshàng dào le* 马上到了 (lit. "on the horse arriving") invokes powerful imagery of gallant warriors and bareback stallions on a windswept plain. It sounds fast, it should be fast, but in reality it probably means your meeting is going to start half an hour late.

Hěn nánshuō
很难说

Translation: It's hard to say.
True meaning: I have no idea; or I know and don't want to say.

An elegant way to dodge any question or curtail any inquiry. Like its cousin *shuōbudìng* 说不定 (can't say for sure), the possible reasons why she isn't saying are infinite. So if you're on a date and this phrase pops up, it could mean you're approaching the promised land. Or, you failed to read between the lines and you're toast—date over.

Yǐhòu zàishuō
以后再说

Translation: Let's talk about it later.
True meaning: I'm hoping we'll both forget and it never comes
                      up again.

Not disagreement, not agreement, not agreeing to disagree. It's a temporary deferment that might not be revisited. This phrase most often comes up when the speaker is …

(a) acknowledging the complexity of a situation and its many variables, or

(b) preventing you from raising a sensitive topic in front of clients, or

(c) clueless on the subject and doesn't want others to know.

It's up to you to figure out whether you're with a sensitive genius or a clever ignoramus.

Yīnggāi méiwèntí
应该没问题

Translation: Should be no problem.

True meaning: Everything is under control OR you're in deep trouble.

A structural engineer could feign confidence in your architectural masterpiece. An accountant might assert that your startup company is not going broke. So how do you know whether to relax or run for the hills? The secret is to listen for the pronunciation of the word *yīnggāi* (should). A short, fast, confident or dismissive answer is much better than long and drawn out. If you hear "*yīīīīīīīnnnnnng gāāāāāāiiiiii méiwèntí*" there's a good chance malodorous excrement is about to hit rotating blades.

I think I really, really like you

Chinese enjoy greeting long-lost friends with the teasing expression *nǐ pàng le* 你胖了 (you've become fat), which derives from an implied compliment from times gone by when being fat meant you must be doing really well. This holdover from the days when starvation was a real threat is reflected in the common greeting *fàn chī le ma* 饭吃了吗 (have you eaten). But in modern China, as elsewhere, prosperity is leading to obesity. So much for the healthy traditional *nóngmín* 农民 (peasant) diet. *Nǐ pàng le* 你胖了 has never been more ambiguous.

In fact, there is a relatively narrow range of expressions that one hears in China on how most people feel about any topic. Chinese in groups do not often stray outside the range of *yībān* 一般 (average), *mǎmǎ hūhū* 马马虎虎 (so-so, lit. "horse horse tiger tiger"), *hái kěyǐ ba* 还可以吧 (okay), *hái kěyǐ* 还可以 (even more okay), *búcuò* 不错 (not bad/pretty good), and *hěnhǎo* 很好 (very good). "I like pizza a lot" is much more common than "I'm crazy about pizza" even from the nut who eats it three times a week.

That said, there are plenty of guys who go around claiming everything is *niú* 牛, short for *niúbī* 牛屄, which literally means the cow's vajayjay, though it's better translated as "awesome" or "orgasmic." You gotta love it—even one of the best Chinese expletives is ambiguous.

Ambiguity in Action

Westerners in English often use a relatively wide range of adjectives to convey what they're thinking, whereas Mainland Chinese tend towards a narrower set of expressions so as to not deprive you the pleasure of reading between the lines.

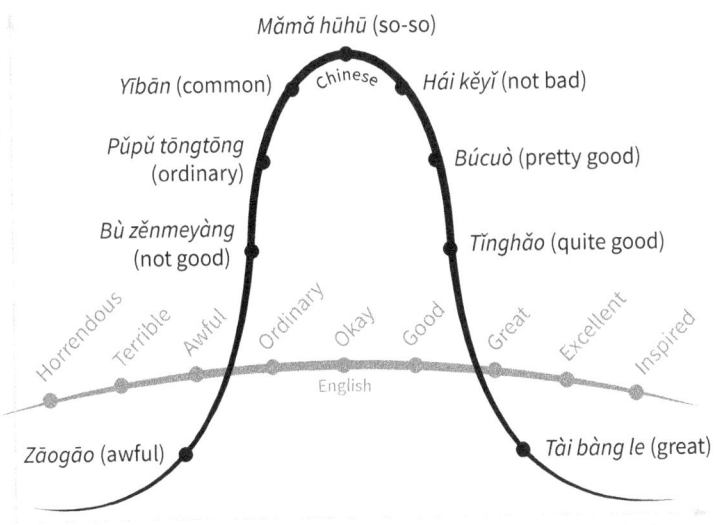

Expert Opinion

Did you know that Chinese people rarely say *"wǒ ài nǐ"* 我爱你 (I love you) to each other? The word "love" feels too strong. If a boyfriend said it to his girlfriend, she might respond: *Nǐ yǒu máobìng ma?* 你有毛病吗? (Are you sick in the head?) as a playful reply even though she might secretly enjoy hearing it. Lovers are more likely to say, *"Nǐ hái búcuò"* 你还不错 (you're not bad), or better yet, *"Nǐ hěn tǎoyàn!"* 你很讨厌! (you're so annoying!) or maybe even, *"Wǒ fēicháng xǐhuān nǐ"* 我非常喜欢你 which sounds like "I really really like you." Yet that might feel quite profound to a Chinese person. If I ever said "I love you" to my father, he would probably ask if I got hit by a car or if I was moving to another planet. For us, when the emotion is real, everyone feels it. There's no need to say it.

Perhaps a little role playing can help illustrate the point. Let's imagine a conversation between a man and a woman, so far just friends, but each hoping it might become something more. Depending on culture, their approach and responses when he calls her up are often quite different:

Western man and Western woman
Ring, ring. Ring, ring.
M: Want to go for a drink?
W: Sure!
M: Okay, see you at 8:00!

Western man and Chinese woman
Ring, ring. Ring, ring.
M: Want to go for a drink?
W: Oh, I'm already at home.
M: Okay, see you next week!
Click.
W: Uh … what just happened? Why didn't he ask me again?

Chinese man and Chinese woman

Ring, ring. Ring, ring.

M: Want to go for a drink?

W: Oh, I'm already at home.

M: It's still early, let's go.

W: But it's kind of cold out there.

M: That's fine, just wear a warm jacket.

W: It's hard to get a taxi now.

M: I'll come pick you up.

W: Okay … I'll go.

Chinese man and Western woman

Ring, ring. Ring, ring.

M: Want to go for a drink?

W: Oh, sorry, I've already got plans.

M: It's still early, let's go.

W: Love to, but I've got plans already.

M: I'll come pick you up.

W: That's very kind of you, but as I said, I've already got plans.

M: But I really want to see you, it would be good for us to hang out …

W: Excuse me, which part of "I'VE ALREADY GOT PLANS" do you NOT understand?

Silence.

M: Don't worry, I'll call you again tomorrow.

Click.

W: Ugh. I've either go to change my number or shoot him.

Same problem when asking a Chinese woman for her hand in marriage. Westerners think it's a one-time offer. You pick the right moment, give it your best shot, and hope she says yes. She said no? Drink yourself silly for six months until it dawns on you there are plenty of other great girls out there. Chinese men, on the other hand, expect "no" to be the first answer. Then it's game on! Let's see how many other creative or romantically mundane ways there are to ask, to wear her down, before she finally gives in. Or so he hopes.

I heard the story of a 30-year-old Chinese man who arrived on a crowded subway platform holding flowers and a diamond ring to ask his Chinese girlfriend to marry him. He had chosen an auspicious date (February 22, 2012) and determined this was the perfect moment for them to start their life together. On bended knee, right in the middle of the platform, he popped the question. And being a good Chinese girl, she politely refused. She must have sounded way too convincing because the would-be-groom fainted in the subway stopping traffic. When he woke up, she screamed: "All you had to do is ask again!" Sometimes the Chinese themselves lose their way in the ambiguity.

Time Travel

Beyond the obvious visual contrasts, there are major perceptual differences between Chinese and English. In the West, people often speak about "putting the past behind us" and "moving forward into the future." Chinese perceive the opposite, with the past in front where it's plainly seen, and the future behind as it's yet to appear. This past-in-front orientation also holds true in Japanese and several other Asian languages. Same same, but different.

The Chinese also have their own method of marking time. Although the Gregorian calendar (the common solar calendar: 365 days a year plus a leap year now and then) is standard across the world, Chinese still follow the lunar calendar, a cultural legacy that has its roots in China's agrarian history. Practically speaking, you only notice the lunar calendar's influence via the numerous "floating" holidays. For example, the Lunar New Year falls on a different day each year and marks the dividing line to a new Chinese birth sign.

Here's where things get tricky. Since Chinese calculate age from life beginning—when sperm meets egg—time in the womb counts as one year. Kids born just before New Year's Day also get to count crossing into the new year as one year. So it's possible for a bouncing baby girl entering the world, after only a few days, hours or even minutes, to hold up two fingers, one for each virtual year of her life so far, and smile for the camera. That's how *xūsuì* 虚岁 (abstract age) compares to *shísuì* 实岁 (actual age).

In China, think "back to the future." Westerners perceive the future as ahead, while Chinese perceive the future as behind us. For example:

qián 前 (front) + *tiān* 天 (day) = day before yesterday
hòu 后 (back) + *tiān* 天 (day) = day after tomorrow

Naming the Nameless

No discussion on Chinese ambiguity would be complete without talking about the *Dao* (also spelled *Tao*), the Chinese "way of being" attributed to the philosopher *Lǎozǐ* 老子 (Master Lao) who lived around 550 BC during the Spring and Autumn Period. The Dao accounts for the long, poetic love affair the Chinese people have with ambiguity. Scholars are unable to agree on the exact dates of his life, or even whether or not he's the real author of the *Dàodéjīng* 道德经 (*The Classic of the Virtue of the Tao*). All of which makes perfect sense. No true Daoist would ever claim authorship of that text.

Daoism contains plenty of wonderful ambiguities, such as:
- In weakness lies strength.
- Force eventually defeats itself.
- Seeking something is the fastest way to not finding it.
- The sage does not boast and is therefore given credit.
- Be humble in the world and eternal power never leaves.

I too find many Daoist truths in my life:
– Maybe is the only sure thing.
– Only optimists see the glass as completely half-full.
– Life is far more the way it is now than ever before.
– I never drink whisky unless I'm alone, or with someone.
– I may be dumb, but I ain't stupid.

The opening verse from the *Dàodéjīng* 道德经 by *Lǎozǐ* sets the stage for 81 transient passages exploring the sublime mysticism of life:

道可道 非常道
名可名 非常名

Dào kě dào, fēi cháng dào.
Míng kě míng, fēi cháng míng.
The Way that can be expressed is not the Everlasting Way. Names that can be named are not changeless names.

Daoists believe that in the perfectly balanced universe, the existence of a quality invokes its opposite. They caution against our human tendency to elevate one quality and reject its opposite, such as when a person's obsession over beauty leads to feeling ugly. In a world of dualities, high and low, light and dark, good and evil, it's impossible to eliminate one without the other. Even attempts to suppress a quality you want to eliminate can backfire; in other words, the more laws, the more thieves.

Me:	What is the secret to inner peace?
Daoist:	Avoiding sharp distinctions between opposites.
Me:	Does this work well outside the monastery?
Daoist:	The next best approach is when neither side of a dichotomy is stressed as absolutely superior, yet both are recognized, leading to a state of complete harmony and inner balance.
Pause.	
Me:	Uh … what was the first one again?

The Daoist concept of *wúwéi* 无为 or "non-doing" is often misinterpreted as inaction rather than its intended meaning of non-interference. In other words, understand that which already is, and go with the flow. Solid advice for anyone living in China.

China can be frustrating from time to time (what foreigners sometimes call "a bad China day") and mystifying to both newcomers and old China hands alike. But as foreigners, we all know that coming in. What could be more foolish than to continue to live somewhere and complain nonstop about it? There are ten thousand things here to annoy you, and a million things here to make you happy. It's your choice.

Where there is opportunity, there is challenge in a sea of ambiguity. Fortunately for us, surfing the wave of ambiguity is easy to learn. It's a balancing act of flowing with your surroundings, while ignoring the reef that can rip you to shreds.

Sorry, There is No Chapter Four

Chinese superstitions at play in our daily lives

钱不是问题, 问题是没钱。

Qián bú shì wèntí, wèntí shì méi qián.

Money isn't a problem; the problem is no money.

ID cards. Street addresses. Phone numbers. Bank accounts. Car plates. What do they all have in common? Each contains a series of digits which can make or break us. Don't take these numbers lightly—your future good fortune depends on it.

The belief that certain numbers have great significance is pervasive and influences both business transactions and personal behavior. Here in Asia, numbers control our outlook on life and perception of our destiny, as well as how others come to see us as potential partners. So no matter how much modern Chinese dismiss these beliefs as outdated superstitions, there's still that nagging worry: "Are all the fours on my car plate an accident waiting to happen?"

It All Adds Up

The paranoia all derives from homonyms and sound-alikes. Eights are auspicious (*pat* 八 = *fat* 发, which sounds like "to make a fortune" in Cantonese), and fours are dangerous (*sì* 四 = *sǐ* 死, which sounds like "to die" in Mandarin). Other numbers vary in the minds of the numerically sensitive, based on word associations in their native dialect.

The Money God is a good guy to have on your side.

My Favorite Mistakes

What I meant:
*Kuài! Sòng wǒ dào **yīyuàn**!*
快！送我到医院！
Hurry! Take me to the hospital!

What they heard:
*Kuài! Sòng wǒ dào **yùyuán**!*
快！送我到豫园！
Hurry! Take me to the Yu Garden!

Máo Zédōng (毛泽东) swept away pesky superstitions and put the kibosh on religion to focus everyone on the practical reality of rebuilding the country. His post-imperial, utopian China had no time for these fanciful feudalistic distractions and social ills. There was also the whole *qiāng gǎnzi lǐmiàn chū zhèngquán* 枪杆子里面出政权 (power grows out of the barrel of a gun) thing to keep people motivated. These days in modern China, religious tolerance is much more relaxed, and traditional superstitions are back and bigger than ever.

Earlier generations of Chinese placed great significance on numerology, infusing art, literature and architecture with deeper layers of meaning through numbers. In ancient China, *jiǔ* 九 (nine) was particularly auspicious because it sounds the same as *jiǔ* 久 (long lasting).

Nines are everywhere: The monk in the Monkey King story goes through *jiǔjiǔbāshíyīnàn* 九九八十一难 (9×9＝81 tragedies); the emperor was called *jiǔ wǔ zhī zūn* 九五之尊 (imperial throne, lit. "nine five's honor") out of respect; the Summer Palace in Beijing has exactly 9999 rooms; and the 9th chamber in heaven *jiǔchóngtiān* 九重天 is the hardest to get into. The saying *jiǔjiǔguīyī* 九九归一 (in the final analysis) derives from ancient calculations on an abacus, where adding one to 99 sends you back to the start (not 100), with Buddhist overtones that once you reach the ripe old age of 99, you may soon return to age one in a new body.

On the other side of the planet around the same time, Pythagoras and his crew of Greek math geniuses were likewise captivated by the power of numbers. As human beings we're hardwired to look for meaning in figures and symbols, even if our ultimate conclusions differ.

News flash: The Cantonese win the award for most superstitious! Hardly a shock. Ask any Chinese. Perhaps it's because their treacherous coastline in southeast China has seen so many fortunes made and lost over the centuries. Money comes fast—just look at Hong Kong—and godly offerings are thought to bring a degree of safety and reassurance. Often the richer someone gets, the more superstitious he or she becomes, which is why we get sayings like these down south:

Yǒu qián de rén shāoxiāng bàifó
有钱的人烧香拜佛。
Rich people burn incense offerings (to keep their fortunes).

Méiyǒu qián de rén suànmìng
没有钱的人算命。
Poor people seek fortunetellers.

So what do they ask?

Wǒ shénme shíhòu kěyǐ yùjiàn wǒ de xīnshàngrén?
我什么时候可以遇见我的心上人?
When will I meet my soul mate?

Wǒ shénme shíhòu kěyǐ fācái?
我什么时候可以发财?
When will I get rich?

Àiya, rúguǒ wǒ sǐ le, dànshì qián hái méi yòngwán, zěnmebàn?
哎呀，如果我死了，但是钱还没用完，怎么办?
Aiyaaaa, what if I die before I spend all my money?

Clocks at home, no problem. Clocks as a gift, lethal problem.

Hong Kong tycoons often shell out millions of dollars for the luckiest car number plates. Plate 2318 in Cantonese *yi sam yat pat* sounds like "easy life and prosperity" and sold for HK$1.7 million even during the 2009 financial crisis. Other popular plates include 26 *yi luk* (easy to be happy), 29 *yi kau* (easy to last forever), 1314 *yat sam yat sai* (for your whole life), and the granddaddy of them all: 18 *yat pat* (prosperity guaranteed) which fetched a cool HK$16.5 million in a 2008 auction. Lucky indeed, especially for the person who sold it.

But dear readers, beware delusions of grandeur. Several years ago, after a few close shaves, an overconfident businessman driving his glorious 888-plated Ferrari in the New Territories crashed into a road divider, tumbled down the hill and burned to death. Maybe he should have chosen 5454 (*ng sai ng sai*, don't die don't die) instead.

Everyone seems to be in agreement across China (and much of the rest of Asia) that the worst number of all is 14, meaning to die, going to die, or guaranteed death. Some choice, huh? With a nod to the West's unlucky number 13, some building owners in Hong Kong magically remove both their 13th and 14th floors, just to be doubly safe.

Enter a Hong Kong residential tower elevator and you'll often discover buttons for floors labeled 3A, 12A and 15B—no doubt alternative universes guarded by daemons and fairies. Other times the 1st floor is renamed the "ground floor" (following British conventions) and the 2nd floor is counted as the 1st floor, so then the 3rd becomes the 2nd and abracadabra!—the dreaded 4th floor becomes the less deadly 3rd floor right before our very eyes. Problem solved.

Whenever a lift whizzes past the imaginary gaps between the 3rd and 5th floors or the double gap between the 12th and 15th floors, I'm taken by cleverness of it all. A property agent can show her clients a breathtaking flat on the "16th floor" without admitting it's only 13 floors up. Sweet—higher rent and nobody dies. So depending on your perspective, apartment 4D at 1441 West 14th Street is either a deathtrap or the bargain of a lifetime. I say, drop that cash and grab that key.

Nowadays, there's a counter trend. Some people are starting to like fours. They say the car plate 4444 is so unique that the miserable number four's bad luck overturns in your favor. Moreover, in music scales, the fourth note (do, re, mi, FA ...) sounds like *fā* 发 (to make a fortune). Go figure.

Expert Opinion

Be careful choosing gifts in China, as there are many sound-alike words to avoid. If you buy an umbrella on a rainy evening date, make sure to bring it home and not give it to your date, because *sǎn* 伞 (umbrella) sounds like *sàn* 散 (to break up). In my native tongue, Shanghainese, the word *júzi* 橘子 (tangerine) sounds like *juézǐ* 绝子 (no descendants) which makes tangerines a terrible gift for newlyweds. Also in Shangainese, *píngguǒ* 苹果 (apple) sounds like *bìnggù* 病故 (to die of an illness) so don't bring apples to the hospital. Never give a *zhōng* 钟 (clock) because people may misconstrue the meaning as *sòngzhōng* 送终 (to pay one's last respects). And if you *suì le* 碎了 (break) a plate especially during Chinese New Year, better say *suìsuìpíng'ān* 岁岁平安 (every year safe) to stop your luck from breaking along with it.

Color Me Obsessed

It's not just numbers. Colors too. Red is the best by miles. The saying *hónghóng huǒhuǒ* 红红火火 (lit. "red red fire fire") describes the Chinese love for energetic events and lavish celebrations. Bright, red and noisy … all good.

The characters for *shuāngxǐ* 囍 (double happiness) and *fú* 福 (good fortune) hanging in a family's home or business are always red, with the latter almost always upside down, meaning *fú dào le* 福到了 (your luck has arrived). We wouldn't want it floating around out there unclaimed. Red also kicks butt for *hóngbāo* 红包 ("red packet") envelopes for gifts of money especially at Chinese New Year and at weddings. Brides almost always have a red gown as one of their multiple wedding day outfits.

The color green signifies environmental friendliness, so it's good almost everywhere … except on hats. Yuan Dynasty lawmakers forced men with a prostitute under their roof to wear a green headscarf or hat. So the saying *dàilǜmàozi* 戴绿帽子 ("wearing a green hat") means your wife's cheating on you.

Whilst we're on the subject of our nether regions…when it's our Chinese zodiac birth year (i.e. Snakes in a Year of the Snake), we're thought to be weak and vulnerable to life disturbances, even disasters. What's worse, other animal signs can take advantage of us. What can we do? Red undies to the rescue! The logic goes like this: *nèikù* 内裤 (underpants) are closest to our bodies. Red invokes fire. Animals are scared of fire. Therefore avoiding attack is as simple as setting fire to our private parts.

Seen and Unseen

The practice of *bàizǔ* 拜祖 (ancestor worship) as an ongoing expression of *xiào* 孝 (filial piety or obedience) is another interesting collision of tradition and superstition. It's done out of gratitude to your parents for having brought you into this world, even when they're no longer physically in it. You can also ask them for protection and other favors in return.

Some Chinese people are fanatical about playing the lottery and believe lucky numbers will make themselves known to us, or that spirits on the other side are able to bless us with the winning number. Indeed, one Chinese man I know purchases tickets using combinations of digits from the birthdays of his favorite deceased relatives. Every day he pesters them, promising not to blow the money if he wins.

His losing streak continued for years, until one day his dead wife took pity and appeared to him in a dream. Excited to see her, he swore to be a better person and donate half the money to charity and the like, then he begged her, "Please, please! What are tomorrow's winning numbers?" His bemused wife shrugged her shoulders and said: "How should I know?"

The *zhāocáimāo* 招财猫 (lit. "attract money cat"), originally from Japan, is locked in a fierce feline struggle for customer greeting dominance.

Despite the persistence of superstition, the ever-pragmatic Chinese swerve towards simplicity, to agnostic caution and to what's traditionally worked. Dèng Xiǎopíng (邓小平) said it best:

黑猫白猫，只要会抓老鼠，就是好猫。
Hēimāo báimāo, zhǐyào huì zhuā lǎoshǔ, jiùshì hǎo māo.
Black cat, white cat, as long as it catches mice, that's a good cat.

A Lifetime in Four Characters

Using idioms to capture an idea's essence in an instant

南辕北辙

Nányuánběizhé

Try to go south by driving your chariot north

Idioms enjoy an exalted status in Chinese language and culture. Pithy expressions, deep in meaning yet elegantly simple, *chéngyǔ* 成语 (idioms) more than any other linguistic construct, provide a unique insight into the past and demonstrate the Chinese preference for practicality. If a truth found any kind of traction over the millennia, trust me, someone inked it onto bamboo and parlayed it into an idiom.

Chéngyǔ are four-character, less-is-more mini-poems providing writers and speakers with instant shortcuts to their deeper meanings. Why elaborate? Just fire one of these laser-guided linguistic missiles into the fray and run for cover.

Not to be confused with *súyǔ* 俗语 (common sayings), *lǐyǔ* 俚语 (slang) or *kǒuyǔ* 口语 (colloquial sayings), *chéngyǔ* hearken back to dynastic times, with many originating in classic literary works whose wording may feel compressed or somewhat alien to the modern reader. For example, *hànniúchōngdòng* 汗牛充栋 taken at face value is "sweaty ox fills buildings," rather than its true meaning of "a collection of books so immense that it's enough to fill a house and make the poor animal (carrying the books) sweat."

My Favorite Mistakes

What I meant:
Bú fù *zhòngwàng*
不负众望
I won't let anyone down
(Trust me, I've got this)

What they heard:
Bù fú *zhòngwàng*
不孚众望
I won't meet anyone's expectations
(Trust me, you shouldn't trust me)

Chinese idioms number somewhere between a thousand (using the strictest classical definition) and tens of thousands. Ray Jackendoff of the Massachusetts Institute of Technology estimates there are over 25,000 idioms in the English language, which makes sense when you consider that the same stuff seems to happen no matter where you live:

Hǎidǐlāozhēn, 海底捞针 (lit. "sea bottom drag needle")
The English "searching for a needle in a haystack" sounds like a piece of cake compared with the underwater Chinese equivalent.

Pāozhuānyǐnyù, 抛砖引玉 (lit. "toss brick attract jade")
When someone in a meeting (never me, of course) tosses out shallow observations hoping to trigger a brilliant pearl of wisdom from someone else.

Shěshēngqǔyì, 舍生取义 (lit. "give life obtain justice")
Dying for a cause we believe in, like free wifi everywhere.

As you might expect, many *chéngyǔ* feature numbers:

Yílùshùnfēng, 一路顺风 (lit. "one road smooth wind")
Have a smooth journey, with the wind all the way. Some people don't like to hear this when boarding an airplane, because downwind takeoffs are problematic, so in that case use *yílùpíng'ān,* 一路平安 (have a safe trip).

Èrsānqídé, 二三其德 (lit. "two three such mind")
To be undecided, or feel half-hearted.

Sānsīérxíng, 三思而行 (lit. "three think then go")
Think thrice before you act. Chinese are three times more careful—in our English version we only advise looking once before leaping.

The idiom *wǔmǎfēnshī* 五马分尸 (lit. "five horses divide corpse") comes from the Qin era method of capital punishment. In modern life, it can be used to mean: if I don't finish this illustration by 8 am tomorrow morning I'll die a very ugly death.

Some *chéngyǔ* make colorful use of animals and plants:

Xiōngyǒuchéngzhú, 胸有成竹 (lit. "breast has success bamboo")
You've got such a brilliant plan, your chest is loaded up with auspicious bamboo.

Guàyángtóu, màigǒuròu, 挂羊头卖狗肉 (lit. "hang sheep's head, sell dog meat")
Buyer beware, man's best friend may be in your shopping bag.

Wǔmǎfēnshī, 五马分尸 (lit. "five horses divide corpse")
The gold standard for dismembering a criminal's body, using not four, but five horses. Why take chances?

And some shed light on love, romance, and relationships:

Àiwūjíwū, 爱屋及乌 (lit. "love house include crow")
When you love someone, you love everything about them,
even their stupid little dog, spiteful cat, and annoying bird.

Qīniánzhīyǎng, 七年之痒 (lit. "the seven year itch")
Enough said.

Chényúluòyàn, 沉鱼落雁 (lit. "sink fish drop goose")
A woman so beautiful she causes fish to sink and geese to
crash from the skies.

The saying
chényúluòyàn
沉鱼落雁 (sink
fish drop goose)
originates from the
legendary stories
of the *sìdàměinǚ*
四大美女 (Four Great
Chinese Beauties),
the most heavenly
eye candy of their
times.

Others become surreptitiously saucy when dropped into the right context:

Wŭguāngshísè, 五光十色 (lit. "five light ten color")
Multicolored is the common meaning, but online it has been twisted into "five naked ten lustful" implying five women showering and the ten eyes of five men watching.

Shuāngguǎnqíxià, 双管齐下 (lit. "to paint with two brushes")
Coming at a problem from two angles, making doubly sure it gets solved. Although in a different context, it might mean "two pipes used together" and bring to mind someone who, um, likes to be with, er, more than one person.

Cosmos, meet Chaos

My personal attraction to *chéngyǔ* derives from their connection with China's fascinating history. Reflecting on these idioms, I can't help but feel a deep respect for the philosophical legacy and wisdom passed down from the master sages such as *Kŏngzǐ* 孔子 (Confucius) and others. Idioms also reveal to us that life in China, at times, is hopelessly chaotic and its long history replete with upheaval.

SNAFU
Some of the many ways to say "all messed up" in Chinese:

yītāhútu	一塌糊涂	*yītiānshìjiè*	一天世界
luànqībāzāo	乱七八糟	*yītuánzāo*	一团糟
luànzāozāo	乱糟糟	*luànhōnghōng*	乱哄哄
záluànwúzhāng	杂乱无章	*língluàn*	凌乱

Way back in the Qin Dynasty, a eunuch minister named *Zhào Gāo* (赵高) plotted to usurp the throne. Fearing the other ministers would oppose him, he devised a way of testing them. In the royal court for all to see, Zhao led a deer into the room and said to the Emperor, "This is a horse." The Emperor laughed and said, "You must be joking." Zhao asked all the ministers, with some agreeing it's a horse, others insisting it's a deer.

After the Emperor went to sleep, Zhao sent his henchmen on a Don Corleone-like operation to dispatch all the ministers who lacked the imagination to see things his way. This is the origin of *zhǐlùwéimǎ* 指鹿为马 (point to deer as horse) meaning a calculated and deliberate misrepresentation.

And if you somehow survive this kind of devious premeditated plot, you must begin *wòxīnchángdǎn* 卧薪尝胆 (lay down firewood taste gallbladder) which means to bear hardships to kindle your vengeance. Don't cross the Chinese: Some have decades-long memories and are willing to sleep on the floor and eat gallbladder rather than forgive and forget.

I often find myself using *luànqībāzāo* 乱七八糟 (messy seven eight terrible) meaning "in great disorder" to refer to street scenes or company politics. Come to think of it, one glance at a newspaper confirms our whole world is *luànqībāzāo*. Buddhists remind us that *sìdàjiēkōng* 四大皆空 (four big all empty), the sensuous world is illusory. So when things become too chaotic, you can always fall back on the maxim popularized by those practical Communists, Mao and Deng, that advises *shíshìqiúshì* 实事求是 (real things seek correct) seek truth from facts.

Expert Opinion

Idioms are a great way to get your point across whilst showing off your appreciation for history and culture. Foreigners should give them a try. Get it wrong and no problem, after all, your're a foreigner! Get it right and you are a genius, so you have nothing to lose. If you mess one up, you can always bounce back with: *qiānlǜyìshī,* 千虑一失 (even a wise person sometimes makes a mistake). And if your friend nails one, you can tease him by saying: *qiānlǜyìdé* 千虑一得 (even a fool sometimes has a good idea). Much of Chinese humor is about how different words connect. For example, there are many uses for the Chinese character *lǎo* 老 (old). If you can convince people to think how you think, then you are a *lǎoshī* 老师 (teacher). If you can get people to do anything you want, then you are a *lǎobǎn* 老板 (boss). And if you can do both, then you are a *lǎopó* 老婆 (wife).

Language Backflips

In character-based systems, the easiest way to widen the vocabulary is to grow words from one-character words to two-character words, which is exactly how the language expanded from the Tang Dynasty's Middle Chinese going forward. And once you've got a two-character construct, it's easy to flip their order and create a *huíwén* 回文 (palindrome):

> *yáshuā* 牙刷 (toothbrush) and *shuāyá* 刷牙 (brush teeth)
> *mìfēng* 蜜蜂 (bees) and *fēngmì* 蜂蜜 (honey)
> *zìsī* 自私 (selfish) and *sīzì* 私自 (secretly)
> *gùshì* 故事 (story) and *shìgù* 事故 (accident)

Chinese palindromes can vary in style and complexity, yet retain symmetry:

> *Shànghǎi zìláishuǐ láizì hǎishàng*
> 上海自来水来自海上
> The water in Shanghai comes from the ocean.

> *Gǎibiàn de huánjìng yǐngxiǎng rénlèi de huódòng,*
> *huódòng de rénlèi yǐngxiǎng huánjìng de gǎibiàn*
> 改变的环境影响人类的活动，
> 活动的人类影响环境的改变
> Changing environment influences people's activity,
> people's activity influences change in the environment.

Funny Haha or Funny Peculiar

Okay, confession time. In my quest to improve my Chinese, I admit to trying the following:

> *Yuánmùqiúyú*
> 缘木求鱼
> Climbing a tree to look for fish.

> *Kōngzhōnglóugé*
> 空中楼阁
> Building castles in the air.

Kèzhōuqiújiàn

刻舟求剑

Cutting a notch in the boat to mark where the sword dropped in the water.

Isn't that last one great? The number of ways to express life's comedy of errors is endless, exceeded only by my natural propensity to err those many errors.

The idiom *huàshétiānzú* 画蛇添足 (draw snake add feet) describes the pointless act of doing something unnecessary.

Idioms often leave their mark by packing a punch line. One of my favorites is: *yǎn'ěrdàolíng* 掩耳盗铃 (cover ear steal bell) which refers to the story of a bungling thief. Unable to relinquish his quixotic quest to possess a massive bronze bell, he decides to smash it into portable pieces. But all that hammering at midnight would wake up the entire neighborhood. His solution? Plug his own ears to muffle the sound.

Another favorite, *cǐdìwúyínsānbǎiliǎng* 此地无银三百两 (lit. "this place no silver three hundred weight measures") mocks someone deathly afraid of losing his fortune. He buries it. And to be extra safe, he marks the hiding place with the sign: "There's no money in this hole." He later returns to discover a new sign: "Your neighbor didn't steal the money."

Careful readers (I mean you, naturally) will be protesting. I implied that *chéngyǔ* are all four characters, even naming the whole chapter after the fact, and I just tried to sneak a seven character idiom past you. Busted. I thought I could *yúmùhùnzhū* 鱼目混珠 "pass off fish eyes as pearls" but you have caused me to *dōngchuāngshìfā* 东窗事发 "have my secret scheme laid bare". Well done, grasshopper. You have learned well.

Idiom dictionaries contain 40,000 to 50,000 entries, 96% of them with exactly four characters. Nonetheless, there are plenty of outliers eager for our attention, such as:

The lofty five-character …
Jífēngzhījìncǎo
疾风知劲草
(strong wind tests tough grass)
Adversity tests one's strength of character.

The erudite seven-character …
Jiělíngháixūxìlíngrén
解铃还须系铃人
(untying the bell still awaits tie-the-bell person)
Don't look at me! Whoever tied the bell to the tiger should remove it.

And the tongue twisting ten-character …
Tiānxiàwúnánshì, zhǐpàyǒuxīnrén
天下无难事，只怕有心人
(below heaven no hard things, only fear have heart person)
Nothing is difficult if you set your mind to it.

I would be remiss if I neglected to mention the *xiēhòuyǔ* 歇后语 two-part enigmatic folk simile, a cousin of the *chéngyǔ*. The *xiēhòuyǔ* starts off with a basic statement, then finishes with a twist:

Jǐngdǐ kànshū–xuéwèn bù qiǎn
井底看书——学问不浅
Reading a book at the bottom of a well–very deep knowledge.

Jiàohuāzi dǎ le wǎn–qīngjiādàngchǎn
叫花子打了碗——倾家荡产
A beggar breaks his bowl–bankrupted.

Zhūbājiè chuān hóng páo–bùlúnbúlèi
猪八戒穿红袍——不伦不类
A pig wearing a red robe–he's still a pig.

Concluding our chapter on idioms in all their delicious complexity, I would like to solicit your assistance with one final imponderable: If those who write novels are called "novelists," and those who craft poems are called "poets," why aren't intellectuals who create idioms called "idiots?"

Fish, Pearl, Coral, and Ocean Go Swimming

The high-stakes challenge of choosing the right name

出问题先从自己身上找原因，别一便秘就怪地球没引力。
Chū wèntí xiān cóng zìjǐ shēnshàng zhǎo yuányīn,
bié yí biànmì jiù guài dìqiú méi yǐnlì.

When problems occur, look to yourself for the reason.
If you're constipated, don't blame the earth for having
insufficient gravity.

The subject of what we call ourselves evokes many passions and provokes lively debate. We all receive a given name from our parents, and after reaching an age when we form an opinion on it—love it, hate it, not sure, my God, what were they thinking?—we have the option of changing it.

I've yet to alter my Western given name, but I've changed my Chinese name several times. Why? Because of my ludicrous self-naming attempts. Why didn't anyone tell me? As we'll see, Chinese find equal pleasure in the selection of an English name, with results ranging from the highly harmonious to the socially disastrous.

Many Chinese take great pride in their *xìng* 姓 (surname), and even though most are just a single character, that character provides a direct link to their family lineage, clan affiliation and colorful history. When first meeting someone, out of politeness you might ask:

Qǐngwèn nín guìxìng?
请问您贵姓？
May I inquire about your precious surname?

And if someone asks you the same question, you should respond:

Miǎnguì xìng Lǐ.
免贵姓李。
Don't be so formal, my surname is Li (or whatever it is).

Even if someone changes their given name, they'll almost always keep their surname.

Take for example the apocryphal story of Rong Yu, a Tang Dynasty poet. Rong Yu earned the admiration of a government minister, who offered his beautiful daughter in marriage, but only if Rong Yu agreed to change his surname, which the minister hated. Rong Yu understood that names are easy to change, while marriage to a wealthy and well-connected goddess on Earth—for your average poet—would be quite a coup.

After much agonizing, Rong Yu shocked his would-be father-in-law by passing on the nuptials to keep his beloved surname. That's how essential surnames are in Chinese identity. Or maybe he was gay and the surname bit was a clever dodge. The truth is lost to antiquity.

Expert Opinion

Chinese consider changing their names for a wide variety of reasons, just like people in the West. Through no fault of your own, you might make people wince or laugh just by introducing yourself. *Liú Chǎn* 刘产 sounds like *liúchǎn* 流产 (miscarriage), *Lài Yuèjǐng* 赖月景 sounds like *lái yuèjīng* 来月经 (get your period), and *Shǐ Zhēnxiāng* 史珍香 sounds like *shǐ zhēn xiāng* 屎真香 (good smelling poop). Or you might discover you share your name with the 290,607 other people called *Zhāng Wěi* 张伟, or the 281,568 people called *Wáng Wěi* 王伟, or the 268,268 people called *Wáng Fāng* 王芳. There's more. The country girl *Zhào Juān* 赵娟 (*juān* means graceful) arriving in the big city can decide to call herself the flashier *Zhào Zhīxiǎo* 赵知晓 (*zhīxiǎo* means knowledgeable) without changing her ID card or angering her parents back home in the village. Or the lovely sounding *Huáng Wǔ* 黄午 (yellow noon) might tire of others misreading her name as *huángniú* 黄牛 (yellow cow, a slang word for ticket scalper) and change it to something totally new.

Are We Related?

Archeologists tell us that the Chinese first started using surnames over 5,000 years ago. As early society was matrilineal, colorful legends described how the earliest rulers came from divine, fatherless births after their mothers sensed the presence of a brilliant shooting star, or glimpsed a powerful flash of lightning, or stepped into a god's footprint. Those stories do sound more poetic than say: "She chased him into the woods, never got his name."

You'll often hear the term *lǎobǎixìng* 老百姓 (lit. "old hundred surnames") tossed around to describe the common people of China. Even though there are over 4,000 Chinese surnames, the top 100 still account for about 85% of the total. Combine the top three surnames—Wang, Li and Zhang—and you've got 21% of the Mainland or roughly 270 million people.

On the other end of the spectrum are the 117 total *fùxìng* 复姓 (double-character surnames) in China, akin to names like "MacDonald" or "von Trapp" in the West. Some *fùxìng* evoke images of a hard life living in villages and working the fields: *Dúgū* 独孤 (alone and lonely), *Yángshé* 羊舌 (sheep tongue), *Zǎifù* 宰父 (kill father), *Húmǔ* 胡母 (pepper mother), and *Tàishū* 太叔 (too much uncle). (I checked the records and was unable to find any "too much auntie" or "spicy mama" out there.) No wonder—despite universal Chinese pride in upholding the family name, multi-character names often get revised to a more standard-sounding surname. All of which goes to show, there's no guarantee any two Chinese with matching surnames share the same ancestors or bloodlines.

Another good reason to change family names was to avoid sharing any of the emperor of the day's given or honorary names, which tended to proliferate with his magnificence. Even writing one was punishable by death. Within the confines of the imperial palace, surnames could be bestowed upon you based on your social status within palace hierarchy, or your clan's origins, or where you lived in the Forbidden City. And rulers could reassign your name as punishment for a crime, so you only have yourself to blame if you wake up one morning to find you're now called "Wu Naughty Fingers".

Or you might ditch the ancestors and change to a new family name because you were wanted—and not in the good way. People on the hit list in one state would flee to another state and change their name to avoid detection. During the Han Dynasty those with the aristocratic surname *Liú* 刘 were exempted from taxes and military service, so you can guess which surname everyone coveted.

Couples in modern China face a much more complex set of choices. Some traditional Hong Kong women add their husband's surname before their maiden name, such as Anson Chan (陈方安生), a former member of the Legislative Council of Hong Kong. But generally wives almost always keep their maiden names after marriage. In the Mainland some mothers decide their "little empress" should carry on her family's legacy (much more tactful than telling your husband his surname is lame). The couple's decision then becomes: Use the father's surname (standard), opt for the mother's surname (not unheard of), or combine the two. So a father named *Fāng* 方 and a mother named *Lǚ* 吕 might call their child *Fāng Lǚ* 方吕.

Bark Like A Dog

You might not realize this, but animals in China make very different sounds from elsewhere (well, on paper anyway):

Dogs go *wāng wāng!* 汪汪

Not *arf arf* or *woof woof*, as in the States.

Cats go *miāo miāo* 喵喵

Whereas in Turkey they go *miyav miyav*.

Sheep only *miē miē* 咩咩

Unlike the assorted bleats, grunts, rumbles and snorts of the vibrant New Zealand sheep.

Horses *yū yū yū* 吁吁吁

In Hungary they *nyihaha*.

Ducks go *gá gá* 嘎嘎

Big Lady Gaga fans, the ducks.

Rooster *ō ō ō* 喔喔喔

With a longer second 'o', not *cock-a-doodle-doo*.

Hens *gé gé dàn* 咯咯蛋

Uh...no idea on that one.

Baby chicks *jījī* 唧唧

They *tsik-tsik* in Urdu.

Cows *mōu mōu* 哞哞

Unlike the Japanese cows which *myor* just once.

Pigs may *oink* in English

But they *gut gut* in Cantonese.

Snakes remain silent here

Problematic if you happen to encounter Moganshan's deadly nocturnal "Seven Step Snake" (that's how many steps you take before it's game over).

Whack! Your name is Aloysius

Given names are even more of an enigma. Let me try to explain this complex subject in one sentence:

(Big breath.) After the surname parents assign either one or two characters as a given name to balance their youngster's yin and yang and/or smooth out inconsistencies in their Five Elements if naming with two characters in a family of same-sex siblings where they often receive identical first characters (i.e. middle of the three) or at least ones which share the same radical like *huā* 花 (flower, for a girl) and *jīng* 菁 (lush, for a boy) to show they are the same generation here using *cǎozìtóu* ⺾ (grass radical) as the shared radical which for example compliments vegetarian astrological signs like sheep rabbits and oxen because they all eat grass which is important to understand. With me so far?

Names have popped up from many unexpected sources—poetry, dreams, occupations, sentiments, weather, seasons, colors, numbers, sounds, plants, and even insects. Others arose from fortune teller ruminations or the first thing mom saw when she went outside after birth.

My Favorite Mistakes

What my friend said:
*Wǒ shì yī ge Rìběn xiǎo **huǒzi**.*
我是一个日本小伙子。
I'm a Japanese young man.

What they heard:
*Wǒ shì yī ge Rìběn xiǎo **hóuzi**.*
我是一个日本小猴子。
I'm a Japanese monkey.

Native Lands

Country names in Chinese come from sound-alike character selections, sometimes leading to interesting literal interpretations:

Country	Pinyin	Characters	Literal
Angola	*Āngēlā*	安哥拉	Safe brother pull
Belgium	*Bǐlìshí*	比利时	Compare advantage time
China	*Zhōngguó*	中国	Middle kingdom
Congo	*Gāngguǒ*	刚果	Strong fruit
England	*Yīngguó*	英国	Hero kingdom
Finland	*Fēnlán*	芬兰	Fragrant orchid
France	*Fǎguó*	法国	Law kingdom
Germany	*Déguó*	德国	Discipline kingdom
Guatemala	*Guādìmǎlā*	瓜地马拉	Melon land horse pull
Ireland	*Àiěrlán*	爱尔兰	Love orchid
Italy	*Yìdàlì*	意大利	Meaningful big advantage
Japan	*Rìběn*	日本	Sun root
Malaysia	*Mǎláixīyà*	马来西亚	Horse come west Asia
Mexico	*Mòxīgē*	墨西哥	Ink west brother
Singapore	*Xīnjiāpō*	新加坡	Newly added slope
USA	*Měiguó*	美国	Beautiful kingdom

There's an ancient story of a mother from Yunnan, hiding by the roadside. She waits for some poor sap to pass, then leaps out and whacks him with a stick until he relents and gives her a usable name for her newborn son. Granted, this is an extreme approach, but it avoids a same-name parade like David William, David William II, David William III and David William Jr.

Parents tend to choose girls' names that sound pretty, gentle, healthy, lucky or virtuous, and boys' names that sound strong, handsome, successful, talented, wealthy or victorious. To help your kid soar like an eagle, name him *Zhǎnpéng* 展鹏 (open wings and fly). Families with all boys who then finally have a girl might call her *Bǎomèi* 宝妹 (treasured sister). Families with all girls may name one *Zhāodì* 招娣 (recruit brother) hoping that will produce the long-awaited son. And mixed-race or western-influenced couples may strive for bilingual phonetic matches, calling their girl both *Xiàlè* 夏乐 and Charlotte.

Moral concepts were in vogue during the Cultural Revolution, so boys were named *Jiànguó* 建国 (build the country) and girls *Hónghuā* 红花 (red flower) or other patriotic monikers. At the same time, acid-munching hippies across the Pacific were dubbing their kids Butterfly, Chakra, Paisley, Moonbeam and China/ Chyna/ Chynna. Isn't life great?

Many Chinese parents leverage the Five Elements to balance their child's name based on surname, birth date and time, or physical variables. Here's the logic: Everything in existence is made up of the Five Elements. Wood is the only living element. Water nourishes Wood. Wood burns, creating Fire. Fire turns to ash, then Earth. Earth compresses to create Metal. Metal contains and collects Water. This is how each element supports (or conversely restrains) another element. So if your surname has Fire, better to select a given name classified as Earth (created by Fire) rather than Metal (melted by Fire) to send your little nipper on an auspicious lifelong journey.

The cosmic explanation is that names have a resonance, positioning us within the universe. In our lifetimes, we'll hear our names spoken hundreds of thousands of times. Each occurrence reinforces a negative or positive magnetic charge around us, which perpetuates the desire for our names to vibrate within our deepest natures. Or maybe I'm just a little lightheaded and in need a bowl of noodles.

Some new Chinese parents sidestep the burden of choosing the apple of their eye's name and with it, the destiny of their descendants, with the clever maneuver and peace-keeping measure of asking the grandparents to name the baby.

Multinationals

Company names in Chinese also originate from sound-alikes:

BMW	*BǎoMǎ* 宝马	Treasure horse*
Coca-Cola	*Kěkǒukělè* 可口可乐	Delicious happiness**
Facebook	*Liǎnshū* 脸书	Face book***
Google	*Gǔgē* 谷歌	Grain song
Johnson & Johnson	*Qiángshēng* 强生	Strong born
Marriott	*Wànháo* 万豪	Ten thousand proud
Mazda	*Mǎzìdá* 马自达	Horse self reach
McDonald	*Màidāngláo* 麦当劳	Wheat of course labor
Microsoft	*Wēiruǎn* 微软	Micro soft
Samsung	*Sānxīng* 三星	Three stars
Siemens	*Xīménzi* 西门子	West door child
Sina	*Xīnlàng* 新浪	New Wave
Toyota	*Fēngtián* 丰田	Harvest field
Twitter	*Tuītè* 推特	Push special
Virgin	*Wéizhēn* 维珍	Maintain pearl
Volkswagen	*Dàzhòng* 大众	Big crowd

* Also called *Bié mō wǒ* 别摸我 (don't touch me)
  for the "BMW" Pinyin initials in the Chinese comedy film
  Fēngkuáng de shítou, 疯狂的石头, aka Crazy Stone.

** Before Coca-Cola came up with arguably the best
  Chinese name of all time, they used to be called
  Kēdǒukěnlà 蝌蚪啃蜡 (tadpoles biting wax).

*** Some netizens use *Fēisǐbùkě* 非死不可 (pun meaning
  "absolutely must die") for a phonetic match.

Big Noses and Foreign Devils

Foreigners using Chinese names is a custom which dates back to the Tang Dynasty. We do it for the same reason Chinese use English names overseas—they're easier for locals to pronounce and a way to connect culturally. In other words, when in Rome do as the Romanians do (sic).

Here's the 3-step process most foreigners follow:

1. Find a Chinese friend with a good vocabulary whom you trust.
2. Together you select a Chinese surname which sounds similar to your Western surname, e.g. Bell = *Bèi*, Garcia = *Gāo*, Maalouf = *Mǎ*, Vincent = *Wēn*.
3. Add two more characters to reflect some positive aspect of your character. Stephanie Smith could become *Shí Jìngyí* 石静怡 (stone, quiet and joyful) and Jason Sutherland could become *Sū Jiéshèng* 苏杰胜 (revive, outstanding and victorious).

Choose wisely and others will be unable to tell—by name alone—whether you're Chinese or not. There are plenty of ways to run amok, however. Some friends have tried to be cute with a novelty name, giving mixed results:

Danny	*Dǎnǐ* 打你	Hit you (not the best way to start a sales pitch)
Eva	*Àihuá* 爱华	Love China
Fabio	*Fāpiào* 发票	The country's ubiquitous tax receipts
Hunter	*Hóngdēngzǒu* 红灯走	Walk when light is red (a popular habit)
Jimmy	*Jīnmào* 金茂	The Jinmao Tower in Shanghai

Keanu	*Jīròu* 肌肉	Muscle
Lorenzo	*Liǎngmǐgāo* 两米高	Two meters high
Roberto	*Luóbotóu* 萝卜头	Turnip head preserved in vinegar
Rose	*Ròusī* 肉丝	Slice of pork

It's worth saying that a foreigner calling himself *Jīnmào* in Shanghai is the equivalent of a Chinese in Paris calling herself Eiffel Tower. Kinda dumb, but at least memorable.

Muffin Man

Why does everyone call me "The Muffin Man?" When I first came to China on business, I remember my Chinese colleagues saying "muffin" this and "muffin" that, then wander off before I could ask what they meant. It took me several weeks to realize they were saying *máfan,* 麻烦 (troublesome) not "muffin". My *suíbiàn* 随便 (casual) colleagues saw my detailed requests as excessive. Perhaps I've been a Muffin Man all my life.

You might find your Chinese friends and co-workers start calling you a name which begins with *lǎo* 老 (old) or *xiǎo* 小 (small). If someone calls you *Lǎo Lǐ* 老李, it doesn't mean you're old, just that you've come a long way, have knowledge to share and people can trust you. It's a mark of respect. Just the same if someone calls you *Xiǎo Wáng* 小王, that doesn't mean you're small, inexperienced or insignificant. It just means you possess youth (compared with the person addressing you) and suggests a certain fondness. Hang in there and maybe someday people will call you *Lǎo Wáng* 老王. It's all good.

Expert Opinion

It doesn't matter what you call yourselves, as soon as you're gone we'll just call you "the foreigner." It's not meant to be mean; it's just the way Chinese see things. Other common terms are *wàiguórén* 外国人 (foreign country person) the standard term *lǎowài* 老外 (old foreign) which is casual and somewhat affectionate. In centuries past, there were terms like *guǐlǎo* 鬼佬 (foreign ghost), *yángguǐzi* 洋鬼子 (foreign devil), and *lǎomáozi* 老毛子 (old hairy/bandit). Sometimes you might hear *dàbízi* 大鼻子 (big nose) if your nose is in fact quite large. Although I can't speak on behalf of every one of the billion plus people in China, as a nation we're pretty fond of foreigners.

Asking for Trouble

Chinese choosing their English names is just as dicey with similarly ridiculous results. The usual process involves searching online dictionaries for an English name or word to match the sound or meaning of their Chinese name. Sounds good in principle, but it's amazing how many people print 10,000 business cards to show off their new English name without thinking to fly it by a native English speaker first.

I can say, hand on heart, that I've had the distinct pleasure of meeting the following Chinese people: Winky, Kitty, Mini, Money, Pretty, Horny, Jovial, Villain, Spoon, Stick, Snow, Rain, Cloud, Rainbow, Moon, Fly, Pearl, Water, Ocean, Ice, Icy, Icicle, Iceberg, Clear, Clock, Credit, Coral, Stone, Wheat, Tomato, Apple, Cranberry, Chlorophyll, Anemone, Jelly, Bone, Bacon, Butt, Milk Powder, Passenger, Show, January, Hotmail, Leader, Legend, Pillar, Titan, Zeus, Alien, Fantastic, Sheep, Wings, Dim, Sim, Sin, Fish, Dolphin, Dragon, Monkey, Mosquito, Virginia (pronounced Vagina), plus a handsome man named Susan, an alluring woman named Ernie, and a muscular guy calling himself Fled, which he insisted is spelled F-R-E-D.

Excuse me, are you kidding?
– No, she's Kidding, I'm Chocolate!
– Hi, my name is Fanny Kok. And she's Fanny Ho.
– Uh … I'm Speechless.
– Speechless, please meet Absidee.
– Absidee?
– Yes, it's spelled A-B-C-D-E.

Whoa, time out. I was just about to open my office door and shout: "Horny! Lucifer! Find Fantastic and Thumbelina and meet me in the conference room in five. Oh, we better invite Trouble too."

When her fiancé's conservative English-speaking parents arrived in China, they asked: "Are you Trouble?" When she assured them she definitely was, the dismayed parents wondered aloud if Trouble might consider changing her name. You know, before the wedding.

A few days later, following their advice, she announced her new name: "Sex". Pandemonium (her sister) erupted.

"Wait, I was only kidding! How's the name Rachel?"

"Rachel is just fine, dear." Reliable sources assure me they're all living happily ever after.

So the moral of the story is: don't worry about courting Trouble in China. And if you can't be logical or reasonable, at least be memorable.

Hungry?

Real life Chinese dishes with their restaurant owner's earnest but all too literal attempts at an English translation:

Fūqī fèi piàn 夫妻肺片	Husband wife lung slice
Qíshān sàozi miàn 岐山臊子面	Qishan noodles smell of urine
Huǒtuǐ zhīshì sānmíngzhì 火腿芝士三明治	Ham sandwich with disabilities
Qīngzhēng tóngzǐjī 清蒸童子鸡	Steamed chicken without having sex
Jīnqiāngyú sānmíngzhì 金枪鱼三明治	Tunny of sandwich
Huíguōròu jiábǐng 回锅肉夹饼	Same tasty dish burger
Tāng húndun 汤馄饨	Dumplings in stupid soup

Never Use the F-Word

How to become more fluent than you ever imagined

只要我们不停下脚步，不管我们
走得多慢都没有关系。
Zhǐyào wǒmen bù tíngxià jiǎobù, bùguǎn wǒmen
zǒu de duō màn dōu méiyǒu guānxi.

It does not matter how slowly you go,
so long as you do not stop.

I am the language master—the Master of Mistakes, that is. People also refer to me as the Chopper of Chinese, Massacrer of Mandarin, Punisher of *Pǔtōnghuà*, and Gouger of *Guóyǔ*. I doubt anyone can match the depth and breadth of my talent when it comes to making a complete fool of myself in the melodic mother tongue of China. I arrived foot-in-mouth two decades ago, and now and then, I still contort Chinese so much that my foot gets back in there.

Yet miraculously, without the natural aptitude for languages some people have, I've become a decent Mandarin speaker. And if I can do it, so can you.

Let's get one thing straight: if you have the time and money to enroll in a fulltime accelerated language program, then go for it. You'll be glad you did. However, if hitting pause on your career isn't an option, read on for creative ways to jump-start your Mandarin practice, stay motivated, and have fun along the road to Chinese language nirvana.

Careless Compliments

A foreigner new to China—phrasebook in hand—decides to pay a compliment, prompting a standard *nǎli nǎli* 哪里哪里 (overpraise) response. However, the literal meaning of *nǎli* is "where?" which for new students can be a source of confusion:

Foreigner   *Nǐde tàitài hěn piàoliàng.*
你的太太很漂亮。
Your wife is very pretty.

Colleague   *Nǎli nǎli.*
哪里哪里。
Overpraise.
(Foreigner hears: Where? Where?)

Foreigner   Beautiful face, nice chest, cute butt …
she's got it all!

From Crawling to Stumbling

No matter where you find yourself on the journey, make sure you prioritize what you most want to achieve both personally and professionally. Set realistic yet flexible goals, adaptable as you progress, resisting the urge to study everything at once.

Learn what you need to say first—your personal core function words—and use Pinyin instead of struggling to decipher characters. What are you most curious about? Grab some interesting vocabulary and get going! Download a language flash card app (or make your own paper flash cards) and challenge yourself multiple times a day. Widening your usable vocabulary is key.

Focus on speaking skills by listening to how native speakers say things. You'll find there's more than one way to say everything, which comes in handy when you forget the vocab you wanted to practice. Most Chinese people relish connecting with language students really giving it a go, so don't be afraid to ask them how to say something. Strive to get your pronunciation exactly right—repeat it back to yourself to anchor it in—or better yet, record your favorite sentences into your phone so you can review and practice them later.

Don't waste time overanalyzing colloquial expressions or struggling over how it works. Mimicking others helps you sound right, so download lots of Chinese language MP3s onto your phone/pod/pad and listen-pause-repeat until you can match their tone and rhythm. Train your mouth to become comfortable speaking with the same absence of tension as in your native language. Embrace becoming known as that guy on the subway who talks to himself.

Challenge yourself with tongue twisters:

Hēi huàféi fā huī, huī huàféi fā hēi
黑化肥发灰,灰化肥发黑
Black fertilizer will turn gray, gray fertilizer will turn black.

Gǒu bèi gǒu yǎo gǒu jiù hǒu
狗被狗咬狗就吼
A dog bitten by a (another) dog will bark.

Shān shàng wǔ kē shù, jià shàng wǔ hú cù
Fá le shān shàng shù, bān xià jià shàng cù
山上五棵树，架上五壶醋
伐了山上树，搬下架上醋
There are 5 trees on the mountain, 5 vinegar bottles
on the shelf,
Cut the trees from the mountain, move the vinegars
on the shelf.

Lín zhōng wǔ zhī lù, xiāng lǐ wǔ tiáo kù
Shè sǐ lín zhōng lù, qǔ chū xiāng zhōng kù
林中五只鹿，箱里五条裤
射死林中鹿，取出箱中裤
5 deer in the forest, 5 trousers in the box.
Shoot the deer in the forest, take the trousers out
of the box.

My Favorite Mistakes

What I meant:
Wǒ yǒu le.
我有了。
I already have it.

What they heard:
Wǒ yǒu le.
我有了。
I'm pregnant.

Same Characters, different meaning.
Another one of those you just have to know.

Give yourself permission to skip any material you're not likely to use in your daily life. Woohoo! Just saved a decade of grinding over boring chapters in outdated textbooks. Some people swear by karaoke as a fun way to learn Mandarin. It pains me to admit that I've yet to complete even one full rendition of *Xīn Tài Ruǎn* 心太软 (*Heart Too Soft*, a popular KTV song) before my friends make a mad dash for the exits. My therapy is helping a lot. Thanks for asking.

Remember, it's vastly better to speak a limited spectrum of words with enthusiasm and some degree of precision, than to mispronounce the entire dictionary.

Perpetual Immersion

We've gotta speak to improve. So grab every available opportunity for real world practice. Spontaneous encounters with native speakers raise your confidence level, expose you to new information, and prove you understand more than you might think you do. Even when you're at a loss as to how to express yourself, you'll start to find creative ways to get your point across.

You might be thinking, "Wait! Not only am I not in China, the nearest Chinatown is hours away! Is this guy asking me to stalk local Chinese families? What if they turn out to be Korean?" To which I would respond, "Whose side are you on anyway?"

These days there are many ways to immerse yourself online, both paid and free, with plenty of talented tutors available for part-time learners. You don't have to relocate to *Běi Dà* 北大 (short for Beijing University) to get a Beijing accent. Shoot for immersion no matter where you live.

Immersion doesn't even need to involve others; it starts within. Develop the habit of naming everything you see during the day in Chinese. It'll push your vocab through the roof. Then when you can, go beyond a single noun for the beverage in front of you—talk about the liquid, its color, the foam, bubbles floating up, the dirty glass, the flavor and everything else about it. Don't know the word? Boom!—there's another flashcard. With a little effort you'll be ripping through your cards, stockpiling precious spoken gems.

Start and finish each day by saying three Chinese sentences to yourself. So as you wake up, talk aloud about what's on your mind and/or what you want to do today, which predisposes your brain towards Chinese. Further deepen your connection with Mandarin by talking about it only in Mandarin—no cheating!

Mute English

There are more than a few Chinese people who can read English but avoid speaking it, aka the "mute" English speakers. Speaking introversion and risk avoidance are the exact opposite of what you want. Reading characters is a worthy accomplishment, but don't get distracted and allow your speaking skills to atrophy.

Character Assassination

Everyone wants to know: do I have to read characters to speak excellent Mandarin? Yes, you do. But not all of them.

You need an appreciation for the characters. Learning the basic stroke orders and the significance of radicals will help you pick up the patterns and accelerate your growth. Having said that, unless you're really into it and have plenty of time on your hands, why pressure yourself to master thousands of characters as you strive to become a solid speaker? Conversational proficiency isn't contingent on the ability to write Chinese.

Of course, if you want to reach the upper echelons of any language, you must be able to read and write. Writing characters helps you remember them better. We're beyond the analog era, so don't feel that you have to write every single character on paper by hand five hundred times. Go digital! There's plenty of Chinese input software out there which allows you to type Pinyin and choose the word you're looking for, as long as you learn to recognize and understand the subtle differences between similar characters. At first, character learning can intimidate and demoralize. Later on, many people find it's their favorite part.

Reading newspapers and magazines in China bores some people to tears. And those channels may not use the vocabulary you want to learn. If that sounds like you, sign up for one of China's popular social media sites, such as *Wēibó* 微博 (lit. "micro blog"), and get your finger on the pulse of China. That's the speedy and entertaining way to learn about hot topics and expand your character comprehension.

Maximizing Your Mistakes

Danish physicist Niels Bohr said that an "expert" is someone who's made all the mistakes which can be made in a narrow field. Malcolm Gladwell, in his book *Outliers*, discusses the need to commit 10,000 hours to become an expert. So reaching the pinnacle of Chinese language proficiency must take about 10,000 mistakes. No wonder I got so good.

You'll recognize your progress by the quality of your errors. When you make a fool of yourself—get over it, it's going to happen—resist the urge to hide it. Smile and play it up! It feels incredible to jabber away without attempting to fix everything. Show others (and prove to yourself) that you're not afraid of the language. It builds rapport. Besides attracting new friends, laughing at our own foibles somehow makes us less like big, hairy aliens from the other side of the world; it makes us real, vulnerable. More human.

温馨提示
مەدەنسى يولۇپ، يېقىنراق تورۇپ تاھارەت قىلىڭ
贴近文明，靠近方便
Close to civilization and convenience

温馨提示
ئالدىغا بىر كىچىك قەدەم باسقىنىڭىز، مەدەنىيلىكتە بىر چوڭ قەدەم ئالغىنىڭىز
向前一小步，文明一大步
Step forward, reflecting civilization

温馨提示
ھەممە نەرسە ئەلا، تازىلىققا رىئايە قىلىش تېخىمۇ ئەلا
一切皆可贵，冲刷价更高
Anything is valuable, especially washing

Online translation utilities yield unpredictable results. For the same reason, when you speak Chinese, converting word-for-word from your native language into Chinese won't work. You need to learn (gradually) to think in Chinese. That way, your mind has direct access to the right phrases and sentence structures.

In case you're curious, the above three "friendly reminder" signs (all parodies of more famous sayings) were photographed in a men's room in Kashgar, Xinjiang, and could be translated as:

1. "Behave better, shoot better (into the urinal)."

2. "A small step forward (towards the urinal), is a big step towards good manners."

3. "Everything is precious, most of all, to flush (the urinal)."

To further your progress using mistake-based learning, get bombed on *báijiǔ* 白酒 (Chinese distilled spirits, about 52% alcohol) and let sloppy Chinese come rambling out of your mouth like a loquacious dipsomaniacal sailor on shore leave. And when an opportunity to slur in Chinese arises, be sure to top it off with the right toast:

Gānbēi!
干杯!
Cheers! Most common toast, which literally means "dry cup" so might be taken as "let's down our drinks."

Hézuò yúkuài!
合作愉快!
To our collaboration! (Said among business partners.)

Xiāngānwéijìng!
先干为敬!
I'll drink first to show my respect. (Said with your superior.)

Búzuìbùguī!
不醉不归!
Not drunk no return, i.e. drink 'til we drop! (Said among friends.)

Acknowledging our lack of perfection to ourselves, not obsessing over what others think or dreading what might go wrong, offers us huge freedom to enjoy learning the language. And for me, that improves my speaking ability. I welcome you to join forces with me and adopt my mantra:

Shuōcuò de yuè duō jìnbù de yuè kuài!
说错得越多 进步得越快!
The more mistakes we make, the faster we progress!

Stay humble. Stay hungry. And let 'er rip! Mistakes aren't social landmines—they're social fireworks.

The Dreaded Blank Stare

I'd just spoken my best Chinese ever. But the shopkeeper is completely flummoxed, staring mouth agape as if I'd asked: "Which way to the nearest pedal-powered particle accelerator?" What I had intended to be an entertaining haggle over a crusty block of *pǔěrchá* 普洱茶 (pu'er tea) has come to a grinding halt in a massive *bù hǎo yìsi* 不好意思 (to feel embarrassed).

Not to worry. It's quite common for locals to miss what learners are saying, even when (hurray!) we actually get it right. Alas, the listener just didn't expect me—the funny looking foreigner—to be speaking her native tongue. She was gearing up for English to come racing out of my mouth and perhaps fretting: I hope my English doesn't embarrass me in front of my daughter. This common misunderstanding shows that increasing numbers of Chinese are keen on improving their foreign language skills. Kudos to them. Fortunately the solution is easy. Just preface your Chinese statement with one of the following mind adjustment phrases:

Qǐngwèn ...
请问 ······
May I ask ...

Wǒ xiǎng wèn yīxià ...
我想问一下 ······
I would like to ask ...

Nǐ kěyǐ bāng wǒ yī ge máng ma?
你可以帮我一个忙吗?
Can you help me?

These short Chinese buffers alert the listener that what's about to come dribbling out of my mouth is going to be in their language, not mine. And regardless of my skill (or lack thereof), my struggle will be appreciated just as much as when someone struggles with my language.

Expert Opinion

Language learning is not a "one size fits all" process, so why approach it that way?
Stay flexible and focus on your current intended target level:

Decent: enough to get by when visiting China.
- Learn your 10 most frequently used survival sentences.
- Become comfortable counting and using numbers.
- Key tools: a basic textbook, plus pen and paper.

Solid: speak well, but don't sweat the characters.
- Build vocabulary, capture volumes of usable words; structure comes later.
- Train your ear and mouth so you have excellent pronunciation.
- Key tools: Skype calls with language tutors, Chinese movies, flash card apps.

Proficient: speak and read with confidence.
- Learn characters and Pinyin together; steady improvement.
- Cover all aspects: vocabulary, sentence structure, grammar.
- Read everything you can get your hands on.
- Key tools: digital dictionaries, Chinese websites, and more flash cards!

Master: translate, learn dialects, pimp out your linguals.
- Broaden your horizons to literature and poetry.
- Simultaneously translate movies, news, tv, and radio.
- Argue and debate with friends using only Chinese.
- Spend four hours a day for two years pushing for brilliance.
- Key tools: all kinds of Chinese media.

The Art of Compliment Dodging

As you progress, you're going to face an inordinate number of compliments from well-meaning Chinese people, including at times, effusive appraisals which far outstrip any honest assessment of your language prowess. Responding with a soft-spoken "thank you" might earn points in the West, but in China, it suggests an oversized ego and overestimated abilities. That's right, the very same abilities they are overestimating on your behalf.

Never fear, these responses will showcase your supreme modesty:

Nǎli nǎli!
哪里! 哪里!
Overpraise! (Really not that good)

Guòjiǎng le!
过奖了!
Overpraise! (It's too kind of you)

Wǒ háiyǒu hěnduō kěyǐ xué.
我还有很多可以学。
There's still so much for me to learn.

Wǒ de lù hái hěn cháng.
我的路还很长。
I still have a long road ahead of me.

Wǒ hái zài "zīzībújuàn" de xuéxí.
我还在"孜孜不倦"地学习。
I'm still assiduously studying it. (Plus bonus points for using an idiom!)

Engaging others with amusing responses leads to more interactions, and generating more personal interactions should be your overriding goal.

Give Us a Break

Know what's really annoying? Foreigners speaking loudly in public places to show off impressive Chinese skills. Please don't be like that. The most gifted communicators choose the language most inclusive of others, without drawing extra attention to themselves.

Never Use the F-Word

Not that F-word. The claim that you are "fluent" in Chinese.

Remember, understatement is a hallmark of Chinese character. So why would you ever want to bring upon yourself the no-win glare of the spotlight, inviting everyone to scrutinize your language skills? It's a sure-fire way to forfeit the respect of all the Chinese people who might otherwise have had huge respect for you. How will you know you're getting good? Let's talk about when you should claim (inner) victory, go out, and celebrate.

Yǔgǎn 语感 is an instinctive feel for a language. It's the bomb. There are standardized tests like the HSK which provide an objective assessment of your skill level, but what we're talking about here is that Zen moment, that inner awareness of personal progress, worthy of a surreptitious fist bump.

The first milestone is a realization that you think in Chinese as you prepare to speak and as you listen. This yields massive benefits in selecting the right expressions and communicating subtleties. You no longer ping-pong between Chinese and your native language, a habit which causes common mistakes and slows everything down. In other words, you've achieved full brain-immersion.

The second milestone to which many foreigners aspire is to become indistinguishable from native Chinese speakers on the phone. Are you able to follow a complex phone conversation with no visual cues or body language? Can you then take it up a notch so that the first time a person you've only spoken to on the phone shows up and is shocked to discover you're a foreigner? In that moment, you know you rock.

The third milestone is to learn a dialect. Many foreigners with excellent Chinese—and typically, Chinese spouses—can draw upon their Mandarin foundations to follow conversations in another dialect. But those taking it to the next level, able to converse in multiple dialects are truly beyond the F-word. They are almost the C-word: Chinese.

In the end, our overriding objective is to use the language to communicate with real people, not become professional students.

Hand Signals

This foreigner isn't trying to ward off vampires at the wet market. He just wants to buy ten (十 shí) oranges.

Beware the Dreaded Sinolinguaphilia

Bionic babblers beware. Speaking copious amounts of Chinese changes how you think, how you behave, even how you converse in your home language. That's right, you become proficient at confusing everyone everywhere you go.

The condition is called *Sinolinguaphilia*, a term derived from the Latin: "Sino" meaning China, "lingua" meaning the tongue, and "philia" meaning love. Not to be mistaken with *Linguabillaphilia*, the fetishistic desire to be tongued by hillbillies.

Sinolinguaphilia is the inescapable feeling of terror as you wake up one morning to discover you're completely *Chinese-ified*. You now eat, drink, breathe, walk, sleep and piss the language, pooping in radicals. Immersion has drowned out all remnants of your former overseas identity. You're now a hybrid of two cultures, able to bounce between both, but not comfortable in either.

Sorry to break the bad news—there is no known cure. If you exhibit any of the following symptoms, you too may be at risk of *Sinolinguaphilia*:

1. You use Chinese word order in your native language, for example, "You what time go airport?"
2. You can no longer say a single *duì* 对 (correct) without letting slip half a dozen: *duì duì duì duì duì duì* 对对对对对对 (correct correct correct correct correct correct).
3. You make the Chinese numeric hand gesture when buying vegetables, just to make sure the vendor really gets it.
4. You speak Chinese by mistake to friends from your home country, drawing stares until you realize your error.
5. You feel compelled to correct the characters in other people's Chinese documents. More people are staring at you.
6. You dream in Chinese, and all the non-Chinese people in your dream (even your granny) answer you back in Chinese.

Fear not. The pace of modern science guarantees the cure for *Sinolinguaphilia* to be imminent. And if I'm wrong, well, how about we start a support group?

"To speak another language is to possess a second soul."

— Charlemagne

Speaking proficient Chinese requires energy and perseverance, but if we're enjoying the process and its many chance encounters, then language nirvana is the journey itself. It doesn't really matter where we end up.

And if over a billion people already speak Mandarin, how hard can it be?

We Let the Boss Die First

Stirring up trouble with dialects, topolects, and slips of the tongue

男怕进错行 女怕嫁错郎。

*Da po kia dip cho hang,
cha ba kia ke cho lang.*

Men worry about going into the wrong career,
women worry about marrying the wrong man.
(in Hokkien dialect)

Imagine driving an hour in one direction to discover people speak an entirely different version of the same language you speak. You drive another hour in another direction and it happens again. Strange coincidence? You order a double espresso to clear your head. And it happens a third time. You drive an hour, same result. Conspiracy theories swirl in your head.

We're talking about Jiangsu province in east China, where Chinese often struggle to follow each others' local dialects. Jiangsu itself has three main dialects, but the on-the-ground reality is much more complex. When describing what they speak, people use city names rather than dialect names, because within dialects there is so much diversity. It all makes sense when you consider that across the vastness of China there are 56 recognized ethnic groups which speak over 80 official dialects. Some comprise multiple sub-dialects with different pronunciation systems, leading some linguists to claim there are nearly 300 living languages spoken within China's borders.

What we have here is a failure to communicate

"Mutually unintelligible" is the buzzword tossed around by the linguist literati to describe two people who can't understand each other's *fāngyán* 方言 (dialect). Even the word "dialect" is controversial. Certain experts prefer the term "topolect" to reflect this spoken disconnect, and to remain politically correct. As the old saying goes, "a language is a dialect with an army."

One could argue that the variations of English spoken in Glasgow, Atlanta, Brisbane, Singapore, and Mumbai are already mutually unintelligible. But after the whisky comes out, those barriers all drift away and our slurring seems to makes perfect sense. The same might be said for Spanish, from its Old World incarnations to its modern variations throughout the Americas.

My Favorite Mistakes: In the elevator

What she meant:
Liù lóu bāng wǒ qìn qìn hǎo ma? (in Mandarin)
六楼帮我揿揿好吗?
Would you please press "6" for me?

What they heard:
Lo low bong woo chin chin how va?
(in Shanghainese).
搂搂抱抱亲亲好吗?
Would you please hold, hug, and kiss me?

All world languages are descendants of earlier languages, further and further back until we were all just grunting at each other. Ah, those were the days! No gerunds, no dangling participles, just eat and avoid being eaten. The million-year journey from *homo erectus* (Peking Man) to the classical written Chinese of the early Confucians was made possible by humans scratching symbols on bones, bronze, and bamboo. What those monosyllabic pictograms actually *sounded* like when given voice, however, still has scholars scratching their heads.

Even the Middle Chinese documented in the official *Qiēyùn* 切韵 dictionary around the year 600 in the Sui Dynasty capital of Chang'an was a "here's what the language should sound like" compromise among the numerous northern and southern dialects. When you want to reunite a country after centuries of fighting, the last thing you need are dialect-driven notions of independence. The Tang poets took things from there, inking verse upon verse of sublime visual art using the "new" Middle Chinese. No doubt their poems were also renowned as potent oratory in the pick-up bars of the time.

Those who fought against a single language in the early 20th century on cultural and egalitarian grounds, such as acclaimed writer Lu Xun, argued in vain for advancement of the dialects so nobody became a second-class citizen. Some even recommended dropping characters altogether and going with an all-phonetic western style system, an idea that never gained traction.

Keep in mind that the "Modern Standard Mandarin" of today is not the root of the language, but rather one of its numerous branches. In the 1950s after the founding of the People's Republic of China and in the aftermath of World War II, the Communist leadership pushed it through as the official language because so many northerners already spoke it. The war had capped off a century of domination by foreign powers, each armed with its own robust single language. Some cadres concluded the only way for the new nation to regain respect was for its people to coalesce around the "common language" of *Pǔtōnghuà* 普通话. After all, its proponents claimed, China's road to language unification would only take one or two hundred years. It was a bold, visionary move driven by political necessity, not that everyone sat down for tea and sunflower seeds when it was done.

Mandarin Chinese is referred to by many names

Pǔtōnghuà	普通话	The common language
Zhōngwén	中文	Chinese (written) language
Zhōngguóhuà	中国话	China's (spoken or written) language
Běifāngfāngyán	北方方言	Northern people's dialect
Běifānghuà	北方话	Northern people's language
Guóyǔ	国语	The country's official spoken language
Guānhuà	官话	Mandarin (ie. government officials') language

Hànyǔ	汉语	The Han people's (spoken) language
Yǔwén	语文	Chinese language and literature
Huáwén	华文	China people's (written) language
Huáyǔ	华语	China people's (spoken) language

English is called "English" pretty much wherever you go, even if it sounds different. But ask Chinese from different places about their language and you'll receive a variety of answers.

Will the "real" Chinese please stand up?

Mandarin has become such a world standard that it's easy to forget there are other beloved, thriving Chinese dialects spoken by well over three hundred million people. Nice round numbers, that's the entire U.S. of A. So it's high time we explore what makes them tick and give our regional dialect-speaking friends some love too.

Yuèfāngyán 粤方言 *(Yue dialect, Cantonese)*

The popularity of Cantonese songs suggests that even though many Chinese can't speak the Yue dialect, they do enjoy hearing it sung by their favorite artists.

Most understand that *Guǎngdōnghuà* 广东话 (Guangdong language) has nine tones to Mandarin's four tones, but we can't just say the written language is the same and the spoken varies. Beyond the obvious great divide between Hong Kong's traditional characters and the simplified characters nearby in the Mainland, Cantonese contains a wealth of colorful expressions, colloquialisms, and street lingo to differentiate itself from its Chinese language cousins:

Kok ko kwok ka yau kok ko kwok ka ke kwok ko
各个国家有各个国家的国歌
Every country has its own country songs.

Yap sat yim sat kam kan kap tsai
入实验室嗱紧急制
You go into the laboratory and press the
emergency button.

Tau tai mo no, no tai sang cho
头大无脑，脑大生草
Big head no brain, big brain with grass
(i.e. he's not so smart).

Cantonese is the home language of Hong Kong, though before the British took over in 1842, the island's inhabitants primarily spoke other dialects. The mass migration of traders and merchants from old Canton into the bustling new colony in the late 19th century was the tipping point. Which is also why most of the Chinese words commonly used in English are taken from Cantonese, such as kung fu, chop chop, gung ho, tofu, dim sum, kow tow, typhoon and brainwash as a literal translation. It isn't surprising—English borrows over half its words from other languages.

Some experts believe the spoken Chinese of the Tang Dynasty was much closer to Cantonese than Mandarin, noting that Tang poetry rhymes better in Cantonese. To account for the similarities between the two, and explain how Tang Dynasty Chinese might have found a home in the South as Cantonese, they reference the Han fleeing from northern barbarians during subsequent dynasties as the geographical route Old Chinese might have taken to becoming Cantonese. The vast northern plains were easily conquered by armies on horseback, whereas the wet southern terrain could be defended by foot soldiers. This area was a sanctuary for more domestic reasons: it was accessible by boat, rice farming was a primary industry, and people could stop moving around. Southeast China's status as home to so many diverse dialects seems to confirm this theory.

Cantonese

Some entertaining Cantonese expressions:

Yau mo kau cho	You've got to be kidding me.
Chi sin ke kwai lo	Crazy foreigners.
Yin kau yin kau	Let's think about it (sounds like: "cigarettes and alcohol" in Mandarin)
Ting nei ko fai	Said when someone is unhappy or has a problem (lit. "block your lung!")
Sang kau cha siu toh ho kwo nei ai	An utterly useless person (lit. "it'd better to give birth to a piece of roast pork than you!")

Many dialects use words which have no Mandarin equivalent and are so colloquial that there is no corresponding character to write them. Therefore, throughout this section, we have only provided characters for Mandarin Chinese.

Mǐnfāngyán 闽方言 *(Min dialect, Hokkien)*

The people of Fujian and Taiwan speak *Fújiànhuà* 福建话 (Fujian language), as do many citizens in bordering provinces. Many people believe the Min region's five to ten language variations are among the most complex in Chinese. Rampant mutual unintelligibility makes life in Fujian quite interesting and explains why your next-door neighbor ("oh, he's just around the mountain") might speak something much different from you.

Linguists tend to segment the Min dialect into the Southern (*Mǐnnán* 闽南), Eastern (*Mǐndōng* 闽东), and Northern (*Mǐnběi* 闽北) versions. Pull together a room of Fujian Min speakers and often the only language they all understand is Mandarin. In these situations, they'll bounce with their homies between Mandarin and their own Min dialect to clarify some points and keep some things to themselves.

Tortoise or Chicken?

My Cantonese friends won't let the book go out without this tongue twister:

Yat man yat kan kwai, chat man yat kan kai,
kui wa kwai kwai kwo kai, ngo wa kai kwai kwo kwai,
kam kau king kwai kwai kwo kai ting hai kai kwai kwo kwai?

一蚊一斤龜，七蚊一斤雞，
佢話龜貴過雞，我話雞貴過龜，
咁究竟龜貴過雞定係雞貴過龜？

One dollar for a tortoise, seven dollars for a chicken.
He said the tortoise is more expensive than the chicken.
I said the chicken is more expensive than the tortoise.
So is the tortoise more expensive than the chicken,
or the chicken is more expensive than the tortoise?

Taiwan is home not only to multiple dialects, but also to many unexpected Mandarin expressions. For example, if you ask for a *tǔ dòu* 土豆 in the Mainland they bring you a potato, while in Taiwan they bring you a peanut. The word *wōxīn* 窩心 means "warmth and happiness" in Taiwan and "disappointing" or "a raw deal" in the Mainland. Even the words for "genuine, pure and authentic" are reversed. In Beijing it's *dìdào* 地道 and in Taipei it's *dàodì* 道地. Perhaps Beijingers and Taiwanese alike sometimes wonder how something trendy in English could possibly be both "cool" and "hot" at the same time.

Fujianhua

Some entertaining Hokkien expressions:

Siao eh!	Hey crazy guy!
Song (shuǎng)	Really satisfying.
Teekey	Stubborn (lit. "metal teeth").
Mai an neh kiasu	Don't be so afraid to lose (used in Singapore.)
Yiao gwee	Greedy person (lit. "hungry ghost").
Lao bat sai	Shed tears (lit. "flowing eye shit").
Mai an neh kuan	Don't be like that.
Wa jia kweh yiam bi li jia kweh bi ka jeh	I've eaten more salt than you have rice (implies I'm older and more experienced).

Note: These expressions are more recognized by overseas Chinese. Hokkien is extremely colloquial and has many variations.

Wúfāngyán 吴方言 *(Wu dialects)*

About 80 million people in Shanghai, Zhejiang, Jiangsu and nearby provinces speak the Wu dialect, making it China's second largest language and the tenth largest in the world. Not bad for a dialect that's no longer taught in schools.

Local parents speak the Wu dialect with their kids from a young age, because they recognize the social benefits in the local community. Often outsiders trying to marry into Wu-speaking families have to learn the dialect for family acceptance. Outsiders also learn it for business advancement. In my experience, very few deals close in Shanghai without two people speaking Shanghainese.

Construction foremen are often super-linguists who juggle a variety of dialects every day in order to communicate with all their workers.

Shanghainese

Some entertaining Shanghainese expressions:

Za sai dee	Crazy! (lit. 13 o'clock.)
Lay	His/her appearance is shocking (lit. "thunder").
Da jay mo	Stacking toy building blocks (slang for shagging).
A la ya ne?	Where's dad? (sounds like "where's my tooth?")
Zetexixi	Naughty and mischievous (lit. "thief laughing")
Ah zz ma wa, ah da xi wa	Similar to saying 鞋子没坏鞋带先坏 *xiézi méi huài, xiédài xiān huài* (shoes were not broken, shoe laces were broken first) in Mandarin, and it sounds strangely like Japanese.
Hangbalangdang jidee?	Similar to saying 一共多少钱? *yīgòng duōshǎo qián?* (how much does it cost?) in Mandarin, this expression sounds funny to Shanghainese, akin to saying "thingamajig" in English.

Babel Reprised

Hakka, Gan, Xiang, Tibetan, Uighur, Mongolian and more. An abundance of language and cultural diversity. Yunnan alone has 55 minority dialects. Here are a few colorful examples from around China:

Sichuan dialect:

The words for "shoes" and "children" both sound like *háizi* 孩子. For this reason, "put shoes on the children" sounds the same as "put the children on shoes." It's all in the context.

Northeast dialect:

Bo le gai ka tu le pi 剥了盖卡吐了皮 is literally "open the top, vomit the skin" but it means you just broke your knee.

Fuzhou dialect:

Nu shan ya zhong is the sound of a Fuzhou person saying, 你长得很漂亮 (you're very pretty), although to a native Mandarin speaker it might sound like 女山压肿—"female mountain press swollen"—an invitation to admire her mountains.

Anhui dialect:

The word *xǐ* 洗 (wash) in Mandarin sounds like *sǐ* 死 (die) in the Anhui dialect. So an Anhui worker, instead of hearing his colleague's polite invitation to shower first, hears: "If you don't die first, then I'll die, or maybe we let the boss die first."

I wonder which of these dialects will survive for future generations to enjoy. Veteran linguist David Crystal writes about the crisis facing our world's six thousand languages, of which half are in serious danger of dying out this century. Distinct dialects with large speaking populations will continue to thrive, whereas in the long term, those similar to mainstream Chinese may be absorbed and forgotten. Does this mean many minority dialects, along with northeast, northwest, southwest, and "under the river" Mandarin, are all doomed to be dragged into the hopper of Modern Standard Mandarin? Perhaps not, if their adult speakers continue to use mostly dialect at home and find a way to preserve sufficient digital content online for future generations. What a pity it would be if we lost these cultural assets.

Chinese everywhere enjoy the pride of speaking their own dialect. You get to say exactly what you want to say and be understood. Your home language is like your favorite dish; if you don't eat it for a while, you miss it. It's a feeling of belonging, something that's forever in you. And yes, everyone thinks everyone else's dialect and accent sound strange. It's all part of our ongoing love affair with languages.

Despite the wide variety of Han Chinese dialects, it's a mistake to say their speakers come from different cultures. The *Chineseness* is much thicker than the geographic bonds which connect Europeans or South Americans. Something about the longest-living culture defies all borders.

Expert Opinion

To learn a dialect it helps if you're good at singing, as most are tone and rhythm dependent. Here are some Shanghainese "melodies" which sound remarkably like other languages:

Sounds like:	Which means:	What Shanghainese hear:
Korean: *Gum sa mi dah*	You're welcome.	*Ge z sa maz ah?* What the hell is that?
Japanese: *Moshi moshi!*	Hello. (answering phone)	*Youshi youshi* Go to hell!
Thai: *La ka tao lai ka*	How much is it?	*La ka ga ne la* It's too hard to swipe the card.

These expressions are so colloquial, it's hard to imagine anyone learning them without full immersion. Speaking dialects requires lifelong learning.

"Perhaps travel cannot prevent bigotry, but by demonstrating that all peoples cry, laugh, eat, worry and die, it can introduce the idea that if we try to understand each other, we may even become friends."

— Maya Angelou

九

The Lingua Franca of the 22nd Century

Will we all be speaking Chinese in the near future?

最明晰的风格是由普通语言形成的。
*Zui míngxī de fēnggé shì yóu
pǔtōng yǔyán xíngchéng de.*

Even the most distinctive style can be
formed with simple language.

anguages are living entities. They inhale ideas and exhale new words, using human beings as their means of expression and expansion.

And now that we've ditched paper for digital, and become willing language evolutionaries and prolific documentarians, the linguistic mayhem is going viral. That's right, we're a long fricking way from etching characters on bamboo. We can now say: I'm online, therefore I am.

Expert Opinion

Internationally-savvy Chinese have the interesting habit of code-switching their language: interspersing English words into their spoken Chinese when discussing a variety of subjects. It wouldn't be unusual to hear these sorts of expressions in a typical Mandarin-speaking office:

Nǐ de boss *yào wǒ bǎ tā de* email address *gěi nà ge* client, *dànshì wǒ méiyǒu nàge* client *de* contact details.
你的boss要我把她的email address给那个client，但是我没有那个client的contact details.
Your boss wants me to give her email address to that client, but I don't have that client's contact details.

Tā de boyfriend *zhēn búshì dōngxi, yǐjīng* call *le tā wǔ cì le, hái méiyǒu* reply, *hái shuō ài tā,* complete *jiùshì* bullshit.
她的boyfriend真不是东西，已经call了他五次了，还没有reply，还说爱她，complete就是bullshit.
Her boyfriend is a real jerk. She already called him five times, still no reply. He claims he loves her but it's complete bullshit.

Cunning Linguists

Every day, we coin hundreds, maybe thousands, of new words around the globe to better move what's inside our heads to the outside. Where our friends laugh at us. But until we evolve telepathy (or aliens drop in with the equipment) words remain our best bet for mutual understanding, appreciation, and basically … not resorting to blowing each other up. So please do me a small favor and give your amazing self a pat on the back. You're expanding our world of ideas without even trying.

Chinese are doing their fair share, pushing the limits of versatility in this age of rapid communication through dialect-jumping and code-switching, without all the precise grammatical trimmings of the Romance languages. In fact, there's a unique vernacular from a very small island, the collision of several distinct native tongues, which remains utterly invincible despite all governmental language police efforts to eradicate it: Singlish!

Its words derive from Cantonese, Hokkien, Teochew, Tamil and Malay. Mixed in with Singapore's native English and Chinese sentence structure influence, this creates a highly combustible and thoroughly entertaining language cocktail. Here are several examples:

I went home and I ting ting ting until I know the answer lor.
I thought long and hard until the answer came to me.

After exams we'll have talk cock sing song session.
Let's have a long chat after exams.

Wah lau! He really ownself go to the party ah?
Oh my gosh! Did he really go to the party by himself?

Oi! Don't anyhow throw the ball can anot?
After kena something den break den you know.
Please don't throw the ball. You might break something.

Even the act of buying a cold drink can bring a smile to the face:

Me: "May I please have a can of Coke?"
Shopkeeper: *"Can cannot, bottle caaaaaaan!"*

It seems our good-humored Singaporean friends take even greater pleasure in their dialect than we foreigners do. Good for them, lah.

The Hardest Problem in Science

Not the Higgs boson particle. Not quantum mechanics and the unified field theory. Not the quest to ban diving in the World Cup. We're talking about the origins of language and what it means to be human.

In their book *Language Evolution*, Morten Christiansen and Simon Kirby contend that to understand ourselves, we must understand language, especially its origins and evolution. This requires experts from a wide range of disciplines, from evolutionary biology to primatology to neurophysiology to psycholinguistics. In other words, some smart mofos.

Chinese Across the Ages

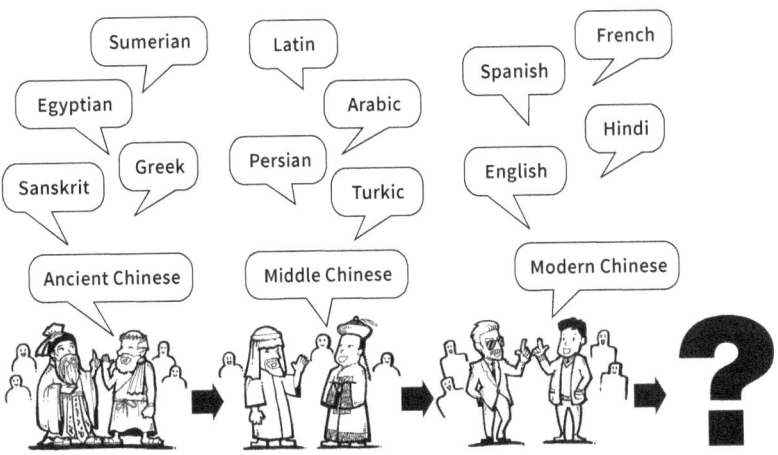

Forging agreement on language evolution hasn't been easy. The debate accelerated in 1859 when Darwin's *On the Origin of Species* hit the bookstores. By 1866, fed up with the litany of wild speculation driven by Darwin's theories, the prestigious Société de Linguistique de Paris banned all discussion on the subject. It wasn't until the advancement of brain and cognitive research in the early 1990s that discussion on the evolution of language as a complex biological adaptation mechanism returned to prominence.

If having a pleasant chit-chat about our linguistic origins in the distant past is that problematic, can you imagine how dicey it might be to embark on a discussion of our linguistic future? Here we go, flying without a net, to explore the monumental question: will Chinese some day become the world's next dominant language?

The Big Eight
The world's top eight languages (in millions of speakers) according to the respected ethnologue.com:

	Total Worldwide	L1 / Native Language	L2 / Second Language
Standard Chinese	1,026M	848M	178M
English	765M	335M	430M
Spanish	466M	406M	60M
Hindi	380M	260M	120M
Russian	272M	162M	110M
Arabic	354M	n/a	354M
Portuguese	217M	202M	15M
French	119M	69M	50M

There are a wide variety of language estimates online, reflecting the vast discrepancy among authorities regarding what constitutes "speaking" a language. For example, some claim there are well over two billion people worldwide speaking English, the vast majority of them second language speakers.

The term "mother tongue" derives from our most basic human connection, mother and child. In this book, *The Mother Tongue*, Bill Bryson tells the splendid tale of how English was the underdog of all language underdogs but overcame its humble Germanic origins to outlast Latin, Gaelic, French, and other powerful champions of the past. Given its meteoric ascension, we would be foolhardy indeed to assume English will dominate the language landscape forever.

So with eyes wide open to the many imperfections in the measurement of language, let's venture onwards through the fog together in search of clues for whether or not English dominance has reached its apex, opening the door for a new world lingua franca to emerge.

Show Me The Money

Before we theorize on whether Chinese will become the most spoken language of the 22nd century, first we must ask ourselves: what constitutes "speaking" a language? Can we claim Lithuanian proficiency if we banter with a taxi driver in Vilnius? Is negotiating the purchase of a cow in Nairobi sufficient for us to say we're speakers of Swahili? And is it enough if we crack a joke in Urdu and get a laugh? It's hard to say.

Mandarin still has a steep path to climb towards worldwide acceptance. Among its current users, roughly 80% are native speakers and only 20% second-language speakers. Compare that with the dominance of English, in which, according to speaker and author Fredrik Hären, we could select any two random people speaking English right now on the planet and there's only a 4% chance that both are native English speakers. But Mandarin's days as an underperforming second or third language may soon be over.

China is starting to gain the same "soft power" influence the British and Americans have used with English for centuries, from missionaries to British Councils and Wall Street English, to Hollywood and the BBC and many others, all of which have contributed to making English today's most accessible language. Confucius Institutes are the most visible example, having been opened in over 90 countries to promote language and cultural outreach programs with China. There are more than 70 institutes in the USA alone offering scholarships, social events, semesters abroad, and "sister city" pairings depending on local market needs. Given the supreme challenge of learning Mandarin, it's only natural for China to standardize and expedite the process.

Stories abound of Western families relocating to China for cultural immersion, parents armed with the knowledge that it's much easier for kids to master the characters and tones if they start early.

Quiz Time!

Which language is most often spoken when:

- Europeans travel to SE Asia?
- SE Asians travel to Europe?
- Russians travel to South America?
- Brazilians travel to North America?
- Iranians travel to Central America?
- Africans travel to Eastern Europe?
- Japanese travel to Western Europe?
- Indians travel to the Middle East?
- Chinese travel to non-Chinese-speaking countries?

The answer of course is English, which explains why global second language learners continue to favor it over Chinese. Among the most populous nations, Indians are learning Chinese (and vice versa) but the numbers aren't huge. Nearly all the top industrialized nations require English as a first or second language, although in practice, not every student receives equal exposure or becomes proficient. That's hundreds of millions of emerging English speakers, which still dwarfs the number of new Chinese learners.

Meanwhile, China has already made English the national compulsory second language in schools, and their hope is other countries will do the same with Chinese. Many progressive countries now offer Mandarin studies in elementary and middle schools, due to its popularity. After returning from China, British Prime Minister David Cameron declared:

> *It's time [for Britain] to look beyond the traditional focus on French and German and get many more children learning Mandarin.*

Should this trend continue to accelerate, the coming decade may well see Mandarin pass a key tipping point as a world language.

The strongest argument for the growth of Chinese language is pure economics. In the decades ahead, China may surpass the United States to become the world's largest economy and speaking Mandarin offers a quick ticket to capitalize on that. We live in a material world and people do tend to follow the cash.

What's more, English could be following the path of vulgar Latin. While Latin left a modern legacy of nearly fifty thriving Romance languages, including Spanish, French, Portuguese, Italian, Catalan, and Romanian, Latin by the 16th century had diminished in mainstream usage outside the hallowed halls of European lawmakers and the Catholic church. And, although English is considered an official language in 170 countries, members of the English-speaking diaspora are happy to use mutually unintelligible vernaculars that bear only a passing spoken resemblance to the Queen's English.

The language now belongs to everyone. The delicious irony of this destandardization of English is that Chinese is racing full speed towards a worldwide standard Mandarin, which if successful, in the distant future, may also cause it to splinter into unimaginable, mutually unintelligible tongues.

What I meant:
Wǒmen yǐqián shì tóngchuāng hǎoyǒu.
我们以前是同窗好友。
We used to be classmates.

What they heard:
Wǒmen yǐqián shì tóngchuáng hǎoyǒu.
我们以前是同床好友。
We used to sleep together.

Xiūsīdùn (Houston), we have a problem

Despite all the effervescent glee in the business press, the "Asian Century" is far from guaranteed. Japan appeared destined for dominance in the 1980s, only to fall back into the pack when limits to its economic model emerged. China has wowed everyone with its achievements over the past four decades, avoiding one economic disaster after another to lift hundreds of millions out of poverty. But what about the next four decades?

Most foreigners seem to think China's too-good-to-be-true economic miracle is destined to crash, while most Mainlanders believe their leaders will continue to navigate the uncertainty and raise the living standards of most citizens. Would I bet against them? No way.

China has a public relations problem. Many outsiders find themselves unable to fully embrace the country in its current incarnation without public transparency, an independent judiciary, and open expression. Modern China has yet to regain the level of cultural affinity of the Tang, Song, and Ming Dynasties. It has yet to strike the cord of compassion and opportunity that attracted past waves of immigrants to the shores of distant lands. Economic supremacy may be won by earning bigger bank balances, but cultural supremacy is earned by winning the hearts and minds of others. Even our centenarian language explorer friend, Zhou Youguang, the creator of Pinyin, doubted that Mandarin (due to its intimidating character script) would ever overtake English as the primary international language.

Here in the future, learning languages is easy— so tell everyone there to just chill!

Simple Pleasures

Becoming highly proficient in Mandarin isn't easy. At every turn we're reminded how hard it is to master a tonal language with thousands of characters.

But who cares? We don't avoid learning to bike just because we might never win the X-Games. We can enjoy cooking classes on day one, without any stress over whether we'll ever become Michelin chefs. Linguists who speak a dozen languages are rarely fluent in all of them, but they learn new ones anyway, just for the fun of it. Even speaking so-so Mandarin can take you all over China, leading to countless adventures and unexpected delights, and the chance to better understand the countless Chinese who'll soon be coming to your country.

I wonder how much longer it will take China to figure out the math. Start with a billion adult native speakers. Buy them smartphones. Give them high-speed internet. And in return, they each teach one foreigner to speak basic Mandarin. Instant lingua franca!

Short of that kind of miracle, English is poised to remain the front runner of the 21st century. But what about the 22nd century and beyond? Your guess is as good as mine, though I anticipate a thriving world of amazing ideas expressed in both broken English and broken Chinese.

Without language, culture would not exist. Words are our means of contemplation, expression and refinement. Speaking a second language, even at a basic conversation level, is the best means available to appreciate its people and realize the richness which life has to offer.

A Brahmin friend once told me that wealth is not measured by our bank balances, but rather by our willingness to answer a traveler's knock on the door, to welcome him or her into our home for a meal and shelter. What a wonderful way to express the wealth of human connection.

"Talk to a man in a language he understands, that goes to his head. Talk to him in his own language, that goes to his heart."

— Nelson Mandela

Resources

Bryson, B. (1990). *The Mother Tongue: English and How it Got that Way.* New York: Avon Books.

Chineseculture.about.com. (n.d.). *The Basics about Chinese Characters.* http://chineseculture.about.com/library/symbol/blccbasics.htm.

Christiansen, M.H. and Kirby, S. eds. (2003). *Language Evolution.* Oxford: Oxford University Press.

Crystal, D. (2010). *The Cambridge Encyclopedia of Language.* Cambridge: Cambridge University Press.

Fairbank, J.K. and Goldman, M. (2006). *China: A New History.* Cambridge, MA: The Belknamp Press of Harvard University Press.

Fallows, J. (2009). *Postcards From Tomorrow Square.* New York: Vintage Books.

Jackendoff, R. (1996). *The Architecture of the Language Faculty.* Cambridge, MA: The MIT Press.

Janich, M.D. (2004). *Speak Like A Native: Professional Secrets for Mastering Foreign Languages.* Boulder, CO: Paladin Press.

Lim, S.K. (2007). *Origins of Chinese Names.* Singapore: Asiapac Culture.

Lonsdale, C. (2006). *The Third Ear.* Hong Kong: Third Ear Books.

Mair, V. (2013 – 2017). *Language Log blog.* http://languagelog.ldc.upenn.edu/nll/.

Miller, G. (2010). *The Pocket Linguist: A Practical Guide to Learning any Language.* Florida: Silver Rocket Press.

Moser, D. (2016). *A Billion Voices: China's Search for a Common Language.* New York: Penguin Random House.

Nisbett, R. (2010). *The Geography of Thought: How Asians and Westerners Think Differently...and Why.* New York: Free Press.

Pan, W-G. (2001). *A Chinese-English Dictionary of Chinese Idioms.* Beijing: Chinese Pedagogics Publishing House.

Penêda, V. (2011, December 6). *Decline of the dialects.* www.globaltimes.cn/content/687342.shtml

Ramsey, S.R. (1987). *The Languages of China.* Princeton, NJ: Princeton University Press.

Seow, J. illus. (2006). *Popular Chinese Idioms.* Singapore: Asiapac Culture.

Wilkinson, E. (2015). *Chinese History: A New Manual, Fourth Edition.* Cambridge, MA: Harvard University Asia Center.

Xi, S-M. (2008). *A New Concise Dictionary of New Chinese-English Idioms.* Shanghai: Fudan University Press.

Yu, Hua. (2011). *China in Ten Words.* New York: Anchor Books.

Zhou, Y-G. (2013). *My Life Story.* Beijing: Contemporary China Publishing House.

References

Chapter One:
The Sound of Somebody Falling Down

"The boat will straighten before it hits the bridge." This line echoes the Daoist view that everything in life develops until the point where things change to the opposite direction, i.e. 物极必反, 否极泰来, "When the negative ends, the positive arrives." In other words, don't panic, because at some point, problems always resolve themselves.

"This will not be my last book!" Zhou, Y-G. (2005). *Bai Sui Xin Gao*. Shanghai: Life Reading Xin Zhi San Lian Bookstore.

"My bedroom is my kitchen." Baidu. com. (n.d.) Zhou You Guang. http://baike.baidu.com/view/65149.htm.

Chinese everywhere share traditions. Fallows, J. (2009). *Postcards From Tomorrow Square*. New York: Vintage Books. Note: Mr. Fallows makes several interesting observations about what it means to be Chinese.

The tragic story of Mr. Yi. Liu He Cai. (2013, December). Yiyiyiyi. http://baike.baidu.com/view/1247745. htm.

The cook's noodles soon became legendary. China.com.cn. (2009, October 28). Biang character creation. www.china.com.cn/book/txt/2009-10/28/content_18784940. html.

Homer Simpson. Groening, M. (1989). *The Simpsons*. Gracie Films. 20th Century Fox Television.

Biang explained. Mair, V. (2010, October 16). *Peace and Harmony*. http://languagelog.ldc.upenn. edu/.

Chapter Two:
A Picture's Worth Ten Thousand Words

Kangxi dictionary. *Kangxi Dictionary*. (2010). Beijing: China Publishing House.

Kangxi Zidian contained 47,035 characters. Nongli.com. (n.d.) *Kangxi Dictionary*. http://www. nongli.com/today/todayxx-114. htm.

2,500 most-frequent characters. Ministry of Education of the People's Republic of China. (1988, January 26). www.moe.edu.cn/publicfiles/business/htmlfiles/moe/s230/201001/75615.html.

Seven micro-movements of the hand to get it exactly right. Professor Xu Guoliang. (1997). Lecture at Shanghai Normal University, from the notes of Katie Lu.

Chapter Three:
Embracing the Ambiguity

Westerners are apt to find Asians hard to read. Nisbett, R. (2010). *The Geography of Thought: How Asians and Westerners Think Differently...and Why*. New York: Free Press, p.60.

Scholars are unable to agree on the dates of Laozi's life. Ivanhoe, P.J. (2003). *The Daodejing of Laozi*. Indianapolis, IN: Hackett Publishing Company Inc. and City University of Hong Kong. Kindle loc 87 of 2238 (Introduction).

The Way that can be expressed is not the Everlasting Way. Society for Anglo-Chinese Understanding. (2006). *Proverbs, 17*. www.sacu. org/proverb17.html.

Chapter Four:
Sorry, There Is No Chapter Four

Plate 2318 sold for HK$1.7 million. Asia One. (n.d.) *Would you pay $320,000 for a car license plate?* http://motoring.asiaone.com/ print/Motoring/Owners/Others/ Story/A1Story20090212-121435. html.

Plate 18 fetched a cool HK$16.5 million. Wu, H. (2008, February 24). *Electronics man pays HK$16.5m to drive off with No18 car plate.* www.scmp.com/article/627443/ electronics-man-pays-hk165m-drive-no18-car-plate.

Chapter Five:
A Lifetime in Four Characters

Hànniúchōngdòng. Liuxue86.com. (n.d.) Han Niu Chong Dong, *What does it Mean?* http://zw.liuxue86. com/z/1321144.html. Note: This idiom originates from a work by the Tang Dynasty poet, Liu Zongyuan.

Over 25,000 idioms in the English language. Jackendoff, R. (1996). *The Architecture of the Language Faculty*. Cambridge, MA: The MIT Press.

Qīniánzhīyǎng. Not a traditional chengyu, just a modern slang expression.

96% of idioms have four characters. Wenda Sohu.com. (n.d.) *Why are idioms four character?* http://learning.zhishi.sohu.com/ question/66070758.html.

Chapter Six:
Fish, Pearl, Coral, and Ocean Go Swimming

The story of Rong Yu. Lim, S.K. (2007). *Origins of Chinese Names*. Singapore: Asiapac Culture, p.80.

290,607 other people called *Zhāng Wěi*. Sina news. (2007). news.sina. com.cn.

Started using surnames over 5,000 years ago. Alchin, L. (n.d.) www.newlyborn.org/surname-meanings/chinese-surnames.htm.

The top 100 still account for about 85%. Newlyborn.org. (n.d.) *Chinese Surnames*

Top three surnames. An, W. (2013, April 12). *No.1 Surname in China gone from Zhao to Li*. www. china.org.cn/china/2013-04/12/ content_28527851.htm.

Kill father, too much uncle. *Zaifu* in a joking sense could mean "kill father," but it originated as an official title. Likewise, *Taishu* originated as the third son among all sons of a king.

Animals in China make very different sounds. Abbott, D. (n.d.) *Animal Sounds.* www.eleceng.adelaide.edu.au/personal/dabbott/animal.html.
Jahnke, M. (2006 December). *Animal Sounds in Different Languages.* http://senselist.com/2006/12/06/animal-sounds-in-different-languages.

A mother from the Yunnan. Lim, S.K. (2007). *Origins of Chinese Names.* Singapore: Asiapac Culture, p.105.

Crazy Stone. Hao Ning (director). (2006). *Crazy Stone* [Motion Picture]. China: Beijing Frontline Production, Focus Films. Warner China Film HG Corporation.

Foreigners using Chinese names dates back to the Tang Dynasty. Fairbank, J. K. and Goldman, M. (2006). *China: A New History.* Cambridge, MA: The Belknamp Press of Harvard University Press, p.78.

Chapter Seven: Never Use the F-Word

It does not matter how slowly you go. Note: This English translation is attributed to a quote by Confucius.

Xin Tai Ruan. Ren, R. (1996). Xin Tai Ruan. Rock Records.

Niels Bohr an "expert" is someone. Mackay, A.L. (1991). *A Dictionary of Scientific Quotations.* London: Institute of Physics Publishing.

The need to commit 10,000 hours. Gladwell, M. (2008). *Outliers.* New York: Little, Brown and Company.

Chapter Eight: We Let the Boss Die First

56 recognized ethnic groups. Chinahush. (2009). *Family Portraits of all 56 ethnic groups in China.* www.chinahush.com/2009/12/06/family-portraits-of-all-56-ethnic-groups-in-china
Dede, K. (2010). *Ethnic Minorities in China.* http://asiasociety.org/countries/traditions/ethnic-minorities-china.

Over 80 official dialects. Penêda, V. (2011, December 6). *Decline of the dialects.* www.globaltimes.cn/content/687342.shtml.

Nearly 300 living languages. Ramsey, S.R. (1987). *The Languages of China.* Princeton, NJ: Princeton University Press.

Spoken Chinese of the Tang Dynasty was much closer to Cantonese. Nan, H-C. (2007). *Nan Huai-chin Speech Collection.* Shanghai: Shanghai People's Publishing House.

Min region's language variations are among the most complex. Fjsq.gov.cn. (n.d.) Fujian Province Information and References. www.fjsq.gov.cn.

80 million people speak the Wu dialect. *Ethnologue: Languages of the World.* (2013). Chinese, Wu. www.ethnologue.com/language/wuu.

Middle Chinese documented in the official Qiēyùn dictionary. Ramsey, S.R. (1987). *The Languages of China.* Princeton, NJ: Princeton University Press, p.122.

Coalesce around the "common language." Ramsey, S.R. (1987). *The Languages of China.* Princeton, NJ: Princeton University Press, p.13.

The crisis facing our world's six
  thousand languages. Crystal,
  D. (2010). *The Cambridge
  Encyclopedia of Language*.
  Cambridge: Cambridge University
  Press.
"Perhaps travel cannot prevent
  bigotry." Angelou, M. (1993).
  *Wouldn't Take Nothing for My
  Journey Now*. New York: Bantam
  Books.

Chapter Nine:
The Lingua Franca of the 22nd Century

Even the most distinctive style can
  be formed with simple language.
  Note: This English quote is
  attributed to Aristotle; the Chinese
  is a reverse translation.
There's a unique vernacular from
  a very small island. Remember
  Singapore. (2011, August 21). *Best
  of Singlish Words and Phrases*.
  http://remembersingapore.
  wordpress.com/2011/08/21/best-
  of-singlish-words-and-phrases.
The Hardest Problem in Science.
  Christiansen, M.H. and Kirby, S.
  eds. (2003). *Language Evolution*.
  Oxford: Oxford University Press,
  pp.1–15.
Darwin's survival of the fittest.
  Darwin, C. (1964). *On the Origin of
  Species*. [Reprint of the 1859 ed.]
  Cambridge, MA: Harvard University
  Press. Darwin, (1964).
Société de Linguistique de
  Paris banned all discussion.
  Christiansen, M.H. and Kirby, S.
  eds. (2003). *Language Evolution*.
  Oxford: Oxford University Press.
Discussion on the evolution of
  language as a complex biological
  adaptation mechanism.
  Christiansen, M. H. and Kirby, S.
  eds. (2003). *Language Evolution*.
  Oxford: Oxford University Press.

English was the underdog of all
  language underdogs. Bryson, B.
  (1990). *The Mother Tongue: English
  and How it Got that Way*. New
  York: Avon Books. Note: Special
  thanks to Mr. Bryson, whose book
  The Mother Tongue inspired us
  to likewise share the fascinating
  evolution of the Chinese language.
World's top eight languages.
  Ethnologue: Languages of the
  World. (2013) Summary by
  language size. www.ethnologue.
  com/statistics/size.
Only a 4% chance that both English
  speakers are native. Hären, F.
  (2013). *One World. One Company*.
  Singapore: Interesting.org.
Confucius Institutes. Confucius
  Institute. (2013). www.chinesecio.
  com/m/cio_wci.
Stories abound of Western families
  relocating to China. Tilton, S. and
  Lee-Young, J. (2012, June 26). To
  Improve Kids' Chinese, Parents
  Head to Asia. *The Wall Street
  Journal*. http://online.wsj.com/
  news/articles/SB100014240527023
  03640804577490671473322992.
David Cameron on learning
  Mandarin. Hutton, R. (2013,
  December 5). Cameron Tells British
  Children to Learn Mandarin, Not
  French. www.bloomberg.com/
  news/print/2013-12-05/cameron-
  tells-british-children-to-learn-
  mandarin-not-french.html.
The Asian Century. Asian
  Development Bank. (2011). *ASIA
  2050: Realizing the Asian Century*.
  Manila: Asian Development Bank,
  pp.11-13.
Zhou Youguang doubts Mandarin
  will overtake English. Branigan,
  T. (2008). Sound Principles. www.
  theguardian.com/world/2008/
  feb/21/china.

"Talk to a man in a language he understands." Bechtel, J., Bundy, D., Winters, G., Thomas, A., Svendgard, B., Kent Wolgamott, L. and Pluhacek, Z. eds. (2013, December 6). Mandela belongs to the ages. http://journalstar.com/news/opinion/editorial/editorial-mandela-belongs-to-the-ages/article_af8087b1-7d0c-5400-992f-319c97c26674.html.

Gratitude

Many thanks to our family members and dear friends who suffered through early drafts of this book without complaint, at least none we ever heard about. 你们的支持无限美！

Deep appreciation to our project team: Sun Zhumin for her many ideas and suggestions; Chua Liwei for her research and story input; John Pasden for his insightful foreword; Rebecca Himpson and Yi Shun Lai for their editorial prowess; Yang Kanzhen for our logo and cover design; Aaron Gu for the book illustrations; Janine Milstrey for the book layout; and Alessandro Gottardo for the cover art. We couldn't have done it without you. 你们的帮助无限大！

Finally to our readers, we extend to you our sincere thanks. We invite you to join us in the worldwide dialog towards cultural awareness and unity in diversity. And if you enjoyed this book, please share it with a friend and post a brief review online. 你们的参与无限好！

About the Authors

Katie Lu 卢海妍
is a native Chinese who
dreams in English. She runs
two businesses: PITT Services
(translation and training)
and EnglishPlus (children's
English learning). Katie and
her team have taught
hundreds of struggling and
genius language students
alike.

Stewart Lee Beck 李渡
has conducted business in
China since the early 1990s
and finds its people and
culture endlessly fascinating.
He cofounded Grassroots
Productions in 2008,
specializing in documentary
and corporate video
production. Stew refers to
his Malaysian Chinese wife as
"the crazy woman who keeps
me sane."

CPSIA information can be obtained
at www.ICGtesting.com
Printed in the USA
FSHW022236140419
57249FS